The Migration Industry in Asia

Michiel Baas
Editor

The Migration Industry in Asia

Brokerage, Gender and Precarity

Editor
Michiel Baas
Asia Research Institute
National University of Singapore
Singapore, Singapore

ISBN 978-981-13-9693-9   ISBN 978-981-13-9694-6 (eBook)
https://doi.org/10.1007/978-981-13-9694-6

© The Editor(s) (if applicable) and The Author(s) 2020
This work is subject to copyright. All rights are solely and exclusively licensed by the Publisher, whether the whole or part of the material is concerned, specifically the rights of translation, reprinting, reuse of illustrations, recitation, broadcasting, reproduction on microfilms or in any other physical way, and transmission or information storage and retrieval, electronic adaptation, computer software, or by similar or dissimilar methodology now known or hereafter developed.
The use of general descriptive names, registered names, trademarks, service marks, etc. in this publication does not imply, even in the absence of a specific statement, that such names are exempt from the relevant protective laws and regulations and therefore free for general use.
The publisher, the authors and the editors are safe to assume that the advice and information in this book are believed to be true and accurate at the date of publication. Neither the publisher nor the authors or the editors give a warranty, expressed or implied, with respect to the material contained herein or for any errors or omissions that may have been made. The publisher remains neutral with regard to jurisdictional claims in published maps and institutional affiliations.

Cover illustration: © Melisa Hasan

This Palgrave Pivot imprint is published by the registered company Springer Nature Singapore Pte Ltd.
The registered company address is: 152 Beach Road, #21-01/04 Gateway East, Singapore 189721, Singapore

Contents

1 Introduction: Brokerage, Gender and Precarity in Asia's Migration Industry   1
Michiel Baas

2 Precarity, Migration and Brokerage in Indonesia: Insights from Ethnographic Research in Indramayu   11
Avyanthi Azis, Rhino Ariefiansyah and Nastiti Setia Utami

3 Brokered (Il)legality: Co-producing the Status of Migrants from Myanmar to Thailand   33
Indrė Balčaitė

4 Understanding the Cost of Migration: Facilitating Migration from India to Singapore and the Middle East   59
Michiel Baas

5 Unauthorized Recruitment of Migrant Domestic Workers from India to the Middle East: Interest Conflicts, Patriarchal Nationalism and State Policy   77
Praveena Kodoth

6 An Industry of Frauds? State Policy, Migration
   Assemblages and Nursing Professionals from India   109
   V. J. Varghese

Index   133

Notes on Contributors

Rhino Ariefiansyah is a filmmaker and adjunct lecturer at the Department of Anthropology, University of Indonesia (UI). His research has mainly focused on environmental issues and how they relate to knowledge production. Since 2009, he has been a member of the Department's trans- and inter-disciplinary research team, which convenes the Science Field Shops with farmers in West Java and East Lombok.

Avyanthi Azis is a lecturer at the Department of International Relations, University of Indonesia, where she teaches in the areas of globalization, development, and migration. Her main research centers on Indonesia's labor outmigration. She currently focuses on the recruitment process and trafficking experiences of Indonesian migrant fishermen. She holds an M.S. in Foreign Service from Georgetown University.

Michiel Baas holds a Ph.D. in anthropology from the University of Amsterdam. He is currently a Research Fellow with the Migration Cluster of the Asia Research Institute, National University of Singapore. Most of his work is India-focused with a specific interest in new middle-class formations. He has conducted extensive research in the field of Indian migration to Australia and Singapore. Furthermore, more recent work focuses on new middle-class professionals in urban India such as fitness trainers and coffee baristas, a topic which he studies through the lens of social and cultural mobility.

Indrė Balčaitė is currently an independent researcher based in London. In 2016, she earned a Politics Ph.D. from SOAS University of London with a research project on Karen migration based on extended fieldwork in Thailand and Myanmar (Burma). A postdoctoral research fellowship at Central European University in Hungary followed. Her academic interests lie at the intersection of political science, social anthropology, and geography and involve migration, borders, ethnicity, and power.

Praveena Kodoth is a professor at the Centre for Development Studies, Trivandrum, India. Recent research examines questions of state policy and political economy in international migration of women from South India. She has also published papers on gender and caste in the context of arranged matchmaking in Kerala and on the reform of gender and marriage in the context of the transformation of matrilineal society in Malabar in the late nineteenth and early twentieth centuries.

Nastiti Setia Utami received her bachelor's degree from the Department of International Relations, University of Indonesia, in 2016. She has spent the past few years working in the tech sector, while running community storytelling projects aimed at youth empowerment in Jakarta. Her current interest evolves around social innovation and entrepreneurship.

V. J. Varghese teaches at the Department of History, University of Hyderabad, India. His areas of interest include modern South Asian history, transnational migrations from South Asia, and making of regional modernities in South Asia. He was British Academy Visiting Fellow at the University of Sussex, Visiting Senior Research Fellow at the National University of Singapore, Research Excellence Visiting Fellow at the Central European University, Budapest and Charles Wallace India Trust Fellow at the University of Edinburgh.

List of Tables

Table 2.1	Top 10 migrant sending areas in Indonesia (annual placement data)	20
Table 4.1	Overview of agencies involved in the research	63
Table 5.1	Emigration clearances given to women from the top 25 sending districts from India, 2012–2017	98

CHAPTER 1

Introduction: Brokerage, Gender and Precarity in Asia's Migration Industry

Michiel Baas

In recent years, there has been a gradual realization that migration cannot solely be understood by focusing on either sending or receiving side. Although increasingly studies of migration take a multi-sited approach, following migrants across the border and from migration decision to ongoing trajectories, an actual focus on what unites sending and receiving sides remains relatively understudied. Studies of transnationalism have partly stepped into this void by showing how various networks act as facilitators and lubricators of migrant flows, but often continue to presuppose an established network, an active diaspora and a certain history to a particular flow of migrants from A to B. However, research increasingly indicates that migrants in Asia no longer strictly rely on such networks and established migrant communities. Due to the commercialization of migration pathways (Baas 2007; Garapich 2008; Lindquist et al. 2010, 11; Surak 2017, 2), the opportunity to migrate has opened up to an ever-widening group of potential migrants. Furthermore, the ongoing formalization and regulation of migration trajectories (Faist 2014; Spaan and Hillmann 2013;

M. Baas (✉)
National University of Singapore, Singapore, Singapore
e-mail: arimba@nus.edu.sg

Kern and Müller-Böker 2015) also makes that increasingly migrants have no choice but to seek out the services of specialist in order to meet stringent rules and regulations. The emergence of a migration industry across Asia needs to be understood in this light.

While research on the migration industry has increased in recent years, most notably following the lead of scholars such as Garapich (2008), Lindquist (2010), and Hernández-León (2008, 2013), there continues to be a lack in empirically rich studies that take the existence of the migration industry as a starting point in order to derive at a deeper understanding of its role in facilitating migration. In particular, its practical, day-to-day functioning remains understudied. A particular problem here is the ongoing demonization of the migration industry (McKeown 2008; Lindquist 2015), which, although not always altogether unjustified, has a tendency to reduce its functioning to the experience of exploitation while glossing over how, especially for low-skilled migrants in Asia, migration is often not even possible without the involvement of agents, brokers and others that make up the industry.

This edited volume brings together a selection of papers which were initially presented at a two-day workshop titled 'The Migration Industry: Facilitators and Brokerage in Asia', held at the Asia Research Institute of the National University of Singapore in 2017. Each of these papers are deeply grounded in extensive fieldwork, building on empirical data gathered through interactions and interviews with brokers, agents and other facilitators of migration. While the experience of migrants with the industry is certainly not disregarded here as well, the papers take a particularly critical approach to migration policy, adjustments and interventions. The picture that emerges from these papers is revealing for the increasing co-dependence on, entanglement of and overlap between migrants, the industry and the state (of receiving as well as sending nation). While migrants are strikingly dependent on the industry for making migration possible, migrants are also involved in the industry themselves, sometimes even envisioning it as a pathway by itself: from migrant to agent or broker. While rules and regulations fuel the need for the migration industry, the state is also dependent on it for the inflow of the right type of migrant. Moreover, the state is actively part in formalizing the industry's role in migration trajectories. While the industry itself depends on the migration desires of its clients, it also plays an active role in fuelling migration desires and creating new pathways. In the following two sections, I will briefly engage with two interlinked questions: *What Is the Migration Industry*, and *What Is Lacking* in the analysis of its functioning (in Asia) so far? In the final section, I will show how the various chapters in this volume provide important insight here.

WHAT IS THE MIGRATION INDUSTRY?

Since the 1970s, there has been a steady increase in the use of labour recruitment agencies facilitating migration to Asia and the Middle East (Lindquist 2010, 123, drawing on Massey et al. 1998). As a term itself, the *migration industry* can be traced to 1977 when it was initially termed 'the commerce of migration', which was held to refer to the activities of a set of intermediaries who profited by offering services to migrants (as discussed in Lindquist 2010). Twenty years later, Salt and Stein would speak of 'a global business' when it comes to the migration industry. Scholars such as Robin Cohen (1997) noted that 'despite the rigorous official control of immigration, there has been an extensive and rapid development of a migration industry comprising private lawyers, travel agents, recruiters, organizers, fixers and brokers who sustain links with origin and destination countries' (Cohen 1997, 163). It was not until 2007 that the term became more commonplace among researchers working on various topics related to migration (e.g. Baas 2007). However, it was particularly Garapich's work on Polish migrants in the EU that set the tone for further conceptualization on the migration industry. Garapich positioned the industry as a 'particular sector of the service economy that stimulates mobility and eases adaptation' (Garapich 2008, 735). Understanding what constitutes the migration industry and how it can be defined remains a topic of debate among scholars however. Various reasons can be pointed at for this.

First of all, there is the terminology itself: while some speak of migration management, brokers and agents, others use terms such migration merchants or subcontractors (e.g. Kyle and Liang 2001). Through such usage a certain divide percolates that distinguishes between legal and illegal migration, the latter mainly referring to practices of trafficking and illegal border crossings while the former is assumed to function within the narrow confines of local and overseas' rules and regulations. The most widely encountered definition is the one by Hernández-León who speaks of the migration industry in terms of an 'ensemble of entrepreneurs who, motivated by the pursuit of financial gain, provide a variety of services facilitating human mobility across international borders' (see also Hernández-León 2013, 25). In his view, it is the migration industry that greases the engines of international migration (2008, 154). It does so by providing and articulating the expertise and infrastructural resources needed for cross-border movements (see also Nyberg Sørensen and Gammeltoft-Hansen 2013, 6). While other scholars have attempted to refine earlier mentioned definitions, the primary discussion has focused on which businesses and actors can be included under this particular umbrella header (e.g. Betts 2013; Light 2013). Fine-tuning the understanding of the migration industry, Nyberg Sørensen and Gammeltoft-Hansen (2013) expand it to include not just service providers that make migration possible but also those so-called control providers such as private contractors performing immigration checks, operating detention centres and/or carrying out forced returns (p. 6). In their analysis of the actors that make up the migration industry, they note the following ones: larger, often transnationally operating companies; agencies and companies facilitating legal migration (sometimes even undocumented); smaller enterprises, typically set up by migrants who have managed to commercialize their own knowledge/experience; clandestine actors (e.g. human smuggling networks, transnational crime organizations, trafficking rings); and finally (the increasing number of) NGOs, humanitarian organizations and migrant associations (pp. 8–10).

What Is Lacking?

Although recent studies and publications by Spaan and Hillmann (2013), Kern and Müller-Böker (2015), Surak (2017), and Cranston et al. (2018) have significantly contributed to the conceptualization of the migration industry, what continues to be lacking is scholarship that engages more empirically driven with the way the migration industry functions on a day-to-day basis. The earlier mentioned demonization or vilification remains an issue here. As Kern and Müller-Böker (2015, 158) note, besides the usual bad practices and fraud cases, 'recruiters perform important roles for the facilitation of transnational mobility and present the necessary infrastructure for labour migration'. Moreover, it could be argued that the industry even plays an important role in making migration safer. 'Brokers are important facilitators in supporting alternative income strategies and new livelihood options for people' (ibid.). Finally, the migration industry seems to play an increasingly important role in migration governance itself.

When Lindquist et al. (2010) suggested to think of that middle space that connects sending and receiving nations as a 'black box' which migration research had a task to pry open in order to understand its functioning, they argued that a focus on brokers is a productive way of doing so. We follow this call here by presenting a selection of papers which do exactly that. By focusing directly on agents, brokers and other commercial and non-commercial actors involved in facilitating migration, the chapters that follow draw attention to the necessity of their involvement, the constraints faced and the risks taken (by migrants as well as the industry itself).

This Volume

This edited volume focuses on three key elements which provide for a deeper understanding of the functioning of the migration industry across Asia: brokerage, gender and precarity. *Brokerage* is utilized here as a shorthand for all these activities that agents (brokers) and others involved in the migration industry are involved in to drive, facilitate and regulate migration. The chapters presented in this volume all engage with various aspects of brokerage, especially in the way policy implementations and adjustments, often specifically meant to protect low-skilled migrants, give rise to various forms of brokerage and the involvement of a migration industry in general. We see *gender* as an increasingly important aspect in the way it structures migration in terms of constraints, opportunities and the direction of trajectories. The feminization of migration is particularly relevant here. Finally, the notion of *precarity* points at how industry, migrants and the state produce, engage with and negotiate the risks imbued, negotiated and taken in migration trajectories, especially those of low-skilled migrants.

In Chapter 2, Avyanthi Azis, Rhino Ariefiansyah, and Nastiti Setia Utami discuss the interplay of brokerage and precarity in the case of (provincial) Indonesia. In particular, the authors do so by problematizing the role informal brokers play in outmigration from the area of Indramayu, West Java. While migration research has frequently highlighted the precarity of migrant workers and how this influences their migration strategies and trajectories, less attention has been paid to the precarity of brokers themselves, and the way this impacts migration flows. As the authors show, the involvement of informal brokers and the way they facilitate migration trajectories is often just one way of generating an income among many. Conceptualizing their brokerage activities as 'moonlighting' helps develop a more nuanced understanding of the commercialization of migration pathways and the scope for making money out of such activities. They situate their analysis within the context of the lessening of other opportunities within the rural area environment of Indramayu which has traditionally always relied heavily on the cultivation of rice for income. By doing so, they point at the way providing brokerage (as an alternative or additional source of income) is deeply embedded in a local context and structure.

With its focus on labour migration from Myanmar to Thailand, Indrė Balčaitė's contribution connects well with the previous chapter in the way that it highlights the informality of brokerage activities. Drawing on extensive fieldwork among Karen migrants from Myanmar who seek to work in Thailand, Balčaitė shows how a private migration infrastructure provides an alternative for as well as an interface to the bureaucratic migration management by both countries. Both documented and undocumented migration of the low-paid variety, deeply rely on expensive migrant brokerage to obtain legal (migrant) work rights in Thailand. Like in Azis et al.'s work, we see what role social networks play in this, and the informal character of activities meant to facilitate migration. Building on extensive fieldwork material, Balčaitė's research sheds light on the omnipresence of brokerage in migration from Myanmar to Thailand as well as the importance of personal networks. Particularly striking is the finding that either documented or undocumented pathways involve similar actors which points at an entanglement of state, migration industry and other stakeholders' related interests.

Chapter 4 then turns to understanding the 'cost of migration' by asking why low-skilled Indian migrant workers pay the amounts they do in order to secure migration to and employment in Singapore. By focusing on migration agents and brokers active in the greater Chennai Region of Tamil Nadu (India), Michiel Baas investigates the costing of migration pathways in order to derive at a deeper understanding of who and what it entails to migrate. As has been pointed out earlier, for low-skilled workers, it is almost unavoidable to make use of migration agents. The case of Singapore is particularly interesting here since it not only involves a migration agent based in India but also one in Singapore itself who functions as the liaison for employers interested in sourcing labour migrants from India. What becomes clear is that the individual amounts quoted for the various costs involved in facilitating low-skilled migration to Singapore do not necessarily add up to the amounts migrants themselves quote as having paid. As Baas argues, the murky nature of migration channels and individuals involved not only makes it nearly impossible for migrants to fully understand what they are paying for; migration agents who source migrants for their contacts in Singapore are also not always aware of what the sub-agents they rely on charge to those who show an interest in migrating.

While generally the industry alleges to closely follow the stringent rules and regulations that were instituted to protect low-skilled migrants, these very same rules and regulation make that it is not always in the interest of agents and brokers to fully know or understand the industry's intricate workings.

The final two chapters in this volume contribute to the picture that rules and regulations to protect low-skilled migrants often contribute to the inherent murkiness of the functioning of the migration industry in Asia. While Chapter 2 discusses this with relation to the practice of moonlighting within the context of facilitating outmigration from Indonesia, Chapter 3 does so in terms of transborder mobility from Myanmar to Thailand. State, industry and other stakeholders are involved in a complex and deeply entangled playing field that makes migration possible 'at a cost' but provides little clarity and transparency to migrants whose decision to migrate is usually influenced by precarious situations at home. Migrating to situations where they are vulnerable to abuse and exploitation and faced with the near-absence of labour rights—especially where it concerns destinations in the Middle East—measures of regulation, protection and intervention not rarely have the opposite effect.

Praveena Kodoth's chapter is a clear example here. Focusing on the unauthorized recruitment of Indian migrant domestic workers for the Middle East, Kodoth takes as a point of departure recent policy measures that have virtually closed the legal route for migrant women. As the author eloquently argues, these policy measures reflect a dominant patriarchal and nationalist logic that speaks directly to the idea of control over women's bodies and the normativity this is imbued with. Strikingly, Kodoth notes that the women public policy supposedly protects have little say in this themselves due to being poor and unorganized. She argues that intensification of controls alongside tacit accommodation of irregular mobility has given impetus to clandestine recruitment which has served to criminalize women while providing impunity to unauthorized recruiters. Even though official or legal recruitment practices for destinations in the Middle East have been restricted, clandestine recruitment for and migration to these destinations continues, though now involving considerably more risk. In general, it can be argued that the protection of migrant workers or the prevention of migration to particular destinations has the adverse effect of making migration riskier, occasionally even more dangerous, and most of all more expensive.

In the final chapter, V. J. Varghese's detailed case study of migration fraud involving large numbers of nursing professionals from the Middle East to India continues Kodoth's line of argument of the entanglement of state, industry and other stakeholders' interests. Varghese shows how complex the relationship and entanglement truly is and how state, industry, stakeholders and migrants themselves deal with and relate to the ever-changing dynamics of the demand for employment overseas and the rules and regulations implemented to facilitate and regulate this. Varghese shows how the governmental regulation of emigration from India and the evolution of its migration industry has been guided by a particular fixity on low-skilled migrants from colonial times onwards. He argues that the configuration and practices of India's migration industry are determined by historically and institutionally situated migration assemblages, which are an outcome of constant and ever-changing interaction between various actors. However, the expansion of the regulative infrastructure, stringent 'migration policing' and new operational mechanisms based on virtual technologies have not been able to prevent corruption and fraud. In fact, it seems that this has even increased as a result. As Varghese argues, migration control has become a precondition for informality. Players within the state apparatus and illegal actors find new ways out of the predicament of the ongoing fine-tuning of rules and regulations, and this in terms neutralizes the intended formal–informal dualism in terms of migration practices.

While the chapters in this volume bring together a number of case studies comprising countries as diverse as Indonesia, Myanmar-Thailand and India with its significant flows of various skilled migrants to the Middle East and Singapore, it does not pretend to provide an all-encompassing answer to the questions it raises about the migration industry. Instead, the intention here is to give impetus to further research and discussion on the developments within as well as functioning of the migration industry across Asia. Changing forms of brokerage and the interplay of factors of precarity and gender seem crucial to this analysis but also require additional reflection to come to a more inclusive and comparative understanding than is possible here. We look forward to seeing how future research will draw upon the findings presented and conclusions reached here and give the migration industry and associated infrastructure a more central place in the analysis of what triggers, facilitates and also constraints migration.

Note on Anonymity and Consent

Throughout the chapters that follow informants' names and sometimes also other details about their lives and histories have been anonymized to protect their privacy. Considering the nature of the ethnographic methods employed, the informed consent was sought of those who participated in the various studies presented here.

REFERENCES

Baas, M. (2007). The mobile middle: Indian skilled migrants in Singapore and the 'middling' space between migration categories. *Transitions: Journal of Transient Migration, 1*(1), 47–63.

Betts, A. (2013). The migration industry in global migration governance. In T. Gammeltoft-Hansen & N. Nyberg Sørensen (Eds.), *The migration industry and the commercialization of international migration* (pp. 45–63). London and New York: Routledge.

Cohen, R. (1997). *Global diasporas: An introduction*. London: UCL Press.

Cranston, S., Schapendonk, J., & Spaan, E. (2018). New directions in exploring the migration industries: Introduction to special issue. *Journal of Ethnic and Migration Studies, 44*(4), 543–557. https://doi.org/10.1080/1369183X.2017.1315504.

Faist, T. (2014). Brokerage in cross-border mobility: Social mechanisms and the (re)production of social inequalities. *Social Inclusion, 2*(4), 38–52.

Garapich, M. P. (2008). The migration industry and civil society: Polish immigrants in the United Kingdom before and after EU enlargement. *Journal of Ethnic and Migration Studies, 34*(5), 701–706.

Hernández-León, R. (2008). *Metropolitan migrants: The migration of urban Mexicans to the United States*. New York: Russell Sage.

Hernández-León, R. (2013). Conceptualizing the migration industry. In T. Gammeltoft-Hansen & N. Nyberg Sørensen (Eds.), *The migration industry and the commercialization of international migration* (pp. 24–44). London and New York: Routledge.

Kern, A., & Müller-Böker, U. (2015). The middle space of migration: A case study on brokerage and recruitment agencies in Nepal. *Geoforum, 65*, 158–169.

Kyle, D., & Liang, Z. (2001). *Migration merchants: Human smuggling from Ecuador and China*. UC San Diego: Center for Comparative Immigration Studies. Retrieved from https://escholarship.org/uc/item/5h24b7j6.

Light, I. (2013). The migration industry in the United States, 1882–1924. *Migration Studies, 1*(3), 258–275.

Lindquist, J. (2010). Labour recruitment, circuits of capital and gendered mobility: Reconceptualizing the Indonesia migration industry. *Pacific Affairs, 83*(1), 115–132.

Lindquist, J. (2015). Of figured and types: Brokering knowledge and migration in Indonesia and beyond. *Journal of the Royal Anthropological Institute, 21*, 162–177.

Lindquist, J., Xiang, B., & Yeoh, B. S. A. (2010). Introduction: Opening the black box of migration: Brokers, the organization of transnational mobility and the changing political economy in Asia. *Pacific Affairs, 83*(1), 7–19.

Massey, D., Arango, J., Hugo, G., Kouaouci, A., Pellegrino, A., & Taylor, J. T. (1998). *Worlds in motion: Understanding international migration at the end of the Millennium*. Oxford: Oxford Clarendon Press.

McKeown, A. (2008). *Melancholy Order: Asian migration and the globalization of borders*. New York: Columbia University Press.

Nyberg Sørensen, N., & Gammeltoft-Hansen, T. (2013). Introduction. In T. Gammeltoft-Hansen & N. Nyberg Sørensen (Eds.), *The migration industry and the commercialization of international migration* (pp. 1–23). London and New York: Routledge.

Spaan, E., & Hillmann, F. (2013). Migration trajectories and the migration industry: Theoretical reflections and empirical examples from Asia. In T. Gammeltoft-Hansen & N. Nyberg Sørensen (Eds.), *The migration industry and the commercialization of international migration* (pp. 64–85). London and New York: Routledge.

Surak, K. (2017). Migration industries and the state: Guestwork programs in East Asia. *International Migration Review*. https://doi.org/10.1111/imre.12308.

CHAPTER 2

Precarity, Migration and Brokerage in Indonesia: Insights from Ethnographic Research in Indramayu

Avyanthi Azis, Rhino Ariefiansyah and Nastiti Setia Utami

OPENING SCENE: AT THE RECRUITMENT OFFICE

It was a Wednesday afternoon in April 2016. Two women came to visit PT Gagah Ayukarso,[1] a private migrant-recruiting agency (widely known

[1] All names presented in this chapter, whether personal or of institutions, are pseudonyms. Our study relies on intermittent fieldwork in Indramayu, which started in March 2016. It also builds upon Ariefiansyah's longer-term ethnographic engagement with Indramayu farmers since 2009. We use participant observation, as well as in-depth interviews with informal brokers and other interlocutors, including returning and potential migrant workers.

A. Azis (✉)
Department of International Relations, University of Indonesia, Depok, Indonesia
e-mail: avyanthi.azis@ui.ac.id

R. Ariefiansyah
Department of Anthropology, University of Indonesia, Depok, Indonesia

N. S. Utami
META Innovation Lab, Jakarta, Indonesia

© The Author(s) 2020
M. Baas (ed.), *The Migration Industry in Asia*,
https://doi.org/10.1007/978-981-13-9694-6_2

as PPTKIS in Indonesia). As they approached, the older woman briefly said, "Here's someone who wants to go (work overseas)." The younger woman was wearing high heels, her face heavily made-up, and her deep red hair worn down. Turning to the potential recruit, the agent on duty, Bapak Suparto, asked: "Non- or ex-?" The red-haired woman was coy and did not look at him. Head bowed, she tinkered with her handbag, and spent a long time not answering. He was referring to whether she had been deployed before. "Non," she finally volunteered. "A non- with dyed hair?" He quipped skeptically. "Usually, it's the exes who have their hair colored." The woman laughed. "Where [did you go]?" he pursued his inquiry. "Hong Kong," she finally admitted. Her name was Euis and had come from the neighboring village. She had completed two contract terms as a domestic worker and was now contemplating a third time. "What work can I do here? I want to work in *sawah*, but I don't have a field, so I have to work abroad. Here it is all headache, there's the water bill, the electricity bill to pay, but no income." The agent asked to see her passport and inquired about her age. When Euis replied 43, he promptly informed her that she had passed the maximum age of 40 for Hong Kong. She looked genuinely surprised that she was no longer eligible but quickly collected herself. She said that she would return again to take her younger sister and a neighbor to the recruitment agency. "They too, want to go abroad."

The snapshot recounted above illustrates everyday reality in Indramayu, West Java, a traditional rice-growing district, which has also been firmly established as one of the main source areas for migrants in Indonesia. The encounter was striking and evokes several questions. First, what to make of the woman who escorted Euis and immediately receded into the background? Apart from the greeting, she only interjected once to relay that Euis was a single mother. Why was she present at all? Was her intermediation necessary or redundant, considering that Euis was someone with previous migratory experience? Equally compelling was the swift, casual way she moved to the role previously occupied by the woman who accompanied her as she promised to revisit and take her turn to escort recruits. Faced with a procedural wall, she did not self-migrate but chose to consult a migration broker. It appears that the practice of intermediation is unceasing and interminable in migration. This is despite the deceitful quality often ascribed to migration brokers, especially those operating in informal spheres. Previous studies on migration brokerage in Indonesia (among others, Spaan 1994; Lindquist 2010, 2012) confirm this impression, but the persistence of brokerage in the Southern precarity in Indramayu does raise important questions about the reason why this is.

The Notion of Precarity

The notion of precarity has been gaining ground across disciplines in recent times. In migration studies, scholars have employed the concept particularly to draw attention to migrants' low-status and low-paid work, often in informal sectors and in an undocumented manner and to showcase the migrant workforce's plight as one of the most vulnerable segments of the global working class (Márquez and Delgado Wise 2011). Guy Standing—whose work helped propel the popularity of the concept of precarity as an analytical tool—claimed today's migrants to be "an integral part of the global precariat" (Standing 2015). We agree that the precarity lens is useful and important for its ability to situate "inequality within broader historical shifts and social structure" (Paret and Gleeson 2016) as well as to shed light on how population movements are contingent upon the deepening inequality, segmentation, and increasing precarization of the global labor market in the neoliberal era (Castles 2015). Nevertheless, as a conceptual tool, its usage has been rather limited, especially as most existing analyses focus on the Global North. Simultaneously, this reiterates both criticisms of precarity as a confined to the specifics of Europe, suppressing experiences of the South (Munck 2013; see also Neilson and Rossiter 2008), and the heavy receiving country bias still not adequately redressed in the study of migration (Castles et al. 2013). From the perspective of the sending country, assertions such as "migrating into precarity" are rather odd since it connotes movement from an un-precarious situation prior to migration. On one hand, this elides the predicament of the South as the main global site of precarity, where it is especially widespread today and historically. As Neilson and Rossiter (2008) points out, "Precarity appears as an irregular phenomenon only when set against a Fordist or Keynesian norm" (p. 54). With specific regard to the context of migration, many studies have shown that migrants are vulnerable in all stages of migration; they experience states of precarity also in the pre- and post-migration stage (often resulting in re-migration). On the other hand, it also offers little explanation as to why people move as presumably people do not move voluntarily into precarious situations. In this study, we offer a Global South/sending country perspective in looking at the link between migration and precarity.

In addition to the industry-specific and collective approaches, Paret and Gleeson (2016) point to the necessity of the sending country approach to advance further research on the migration, precarity, agency nexus. For the purpose of this study, we put less emphasis on agency. Partially, this owes to the positioning of precarity in our respective studies; Paret and Gleeson examine migrant experience to better understand precarity, while our focus remains on understanding migration or, more specifically, the migration industry.

Located at the meso-structural level, the migration industry can be understood as one of a number of intermediate mechanisms relating to the micro- to the macrostructures of migration (Castles et al. 2013), or conceptualized as "the broad array of both legal and clandestine actors linked to the facilitation of international migration" (Sørensen 2012, 61). By migration industry, we mean the actors/mechanisms that contribute to the perpetuation of movements (in this case, from the sending country), not the specific sectors relying on immigrant workforce that Paret and Gleeson (2016) illuminate in their approach. In turning attention to the industry, we assert that focusing attention on migrants alone is insufficient. Rather than specifically directing it toward migrants alone, the precarity lens becomes more insightful when also employed in investigating recruiters and the recruitment process as a whole. Paret and Gleeson see the central significance of the precarity concept in its ability to connect the micro and the macro, i.e., situating inequality experiences of insecurity and vulnerability within historically and geographically specific contexts. Centering attention on precarity as an important attribute of migrant recruiters allows for a more holistic analysis, which does not lose sight of structure and the inequality deep-seated within it. In turn, this framing enables us to withhold passing moral judgment towards these intermediaries. Instead of portraying them as inherently bad or predatory, we see their actions and decisions as contextualized and embedded in the circumstances and constraints of their society, as well as Indramayu's specifity as a place.

While recent explorations on migration industry have begun to look at the relationship between migration brokerage and precarity, the focus has remained on intermediaries' participation in the (co-)production of migrants as precarious subjects (Deshingkar 2018). Not much investigation has been directed at how intermediaries' precarity influences migration. We build our analysis on Lindquist (2010, 2012), expanding on an aspect less discussed in his work (perhaps due to his leaning more toward the labor market approach), namely the "moonlighting" nature of recruiters' involvement with the migration process. Lindquist' insight is instructive as it allows a more refined consideration of commerciality, which a structuralist approach emphasizes (Cranston et al. 2018). It gives an opening to important discussion about how, even if the profit is insubstantial, migrating others presents a real opportunity for livelihood and thus its perpetuation.

Attention to recruiters' own precarious situation could be a way to further another meso-level theorization, i.e., the New Economics Labor of Migration (NELM), with its focus on households' use of migration as a strategy to diversify livelihoods. Here, household is often understood to be that of the migrant; however, Indramayu provides evidence that non-migrating households also utilize migration, i.e., their "migrating others" as an occupation and thus as a source of income. There is thus a "shared precarity" in Indramayu which contributes to perpetuation of the labor migration industry, as both migrant and non-migrant household rely on migration to spread out alternatives for survival.

This Chapter

The organization of this chapter is as follows. First, we embed the understanding of precarity in the historical context of the South before proceeding to a sketch of precariousness in the ethnographic site, Indramayu. In the main discussion, our analysis begins by expanding the risks that brokers bear, denoting the conditions of their precarity, namely the legal stigma, occupational risks, and informalization of their work. We then move on to pertinent issues not dwelt upon in Lindquist' work, namely: (1) elaboration of the income-generating aspect entailed in the intermediation of migration, i.e., brokering as a livelihood; and (2) discussion of the thin, permeable boundary between migration and brokerage—delineating the whole migration enterprise as something intimate. With regard to the first, the focus is on brokerage as a result of labor precarity. Brokering is but an odd job among many which locals in Indramayu pursue, and it does not always translate into handsome profit-making. Indeed, some brokers continue living precarious lives despite long years of migrating others. Expounding the second point, we unpack locals' transition into becoming brokers, looking more closely at the following: route to brokering, migrating close relatives, downplaying of brokerage, and conception of migrating others as helping. Elaborating the route to brokering further, the final segment reflects on the feminization of brokerage as we contemplate the role and relative "success" of women, compared to men, in carving "careers" as migration brokers.

Conceptual and Historical Framework: Indramayu as a Site of Southern Precarity

In delineating precarious work in the Asian context, Kalleberg and Hewison (2013) suggest the following definition by Vosko (2010, 2), "uncertainty, instability, and insecurity of work in which employees bear the risks of work (as opposed to businesses or the government) and receive limited social benefits and statutory entitlements." While we find the attention to risk helpful, its conceptualization remains unsatisfactory. In this chapter, we seek to complement the notion of labor precarity by situating it in Indramayu's concrete historical and geographical embeddedness to trace the processes that render work less secure and lead to locals' complex (off-farming) livelihood strategies.

In this regard, Indramayu's narrative breaks from the dominant Northern account on capitalist restructuring and reconfiguration of global labor, which tends to emphasize the role of corporations in bringing about precarization (Delgado-Wise 2015). Indramayu's specificity as a place indicates it is more apt to anchor understanding of precarity and migration on the (re-)organization of agrarian production, in which the state, in addition to corporations, was also a central player. We agree with Munck (2013) in asserting that, "The Southern experience of precarity is marked by the nature of the post-colonial state and later, by the developmental state where this has emerged" (p. 752). Lee and Kofman (2012) similarly contend that one of the focal points of (non-Northern) precarity politics is that it is "often an integral part of the development strategies of states and international financial institutions, rather than the natural corporate response to global market competition."

As Munck makes clear, informalization and precarious existence did not emerge with the 2008/2009 crisis. For Indonesia, it did not start with the 1997/1998 crisis, either. Munck's more careful reading of the global labor timeline reminds us that worldwide the size of the working class doubled in 1975–1995. Whereas Lindquist concentrates his analyses on the post-1998 era, we find it is necessary to stretch the analytical chronology a few decades further, to the year 1970, as it simultaneously marks a turning point in Indonesia's formulation of policies on rice production (Hansen 1972) and the beginning of the country's policy of labor outmigration. By incorporating Indramayu's ecological crisis in elaborating conditions of precarity, we affirm that "pure" economic consideration alone is not sufficient to explain the drive for migration. As Hugo (2000a, 2000b) notes in his study of the 1997/1998 Asian economic crisis the patchy effects of economic hardship on people movements. Tracing back the timeline to the Green Revolution, we aim to illuminate how adoption of pro-market policies led to the making of precarity in rural areas. In reconstructing our conceptualization of Indramayu's Southern precarity, we further take Munck's advice to pay attention to the dispossession process (Li 2010).

Green Revolution and Its Aftermath

Located in the northern coastal plain of West Java, the region constituting Indramayu regency is traditionally a major rice-producing area. Latest available data from the agricultural office cite Indramayu's annual rice production at more than 1.4 million tons (BPS Indramayu 2016). Most of this output goes to other regions, including the capital of Jakarta. Only 250,000 tons of Indramayu's total rice production goes to local market for intra-region consumption. Stretched over an area of 204,000 hectares, 54.3% (110,877 hectares) of the land is used for wet-rice cultivation (*sawah*). Due to its low land nature, rice-growing in Indramayu is seasonal as water supplies are limited. Unlike its appropriation-resistant uplands, the practice of "escape agriculture" (Scott 2009) is not feasible. The societal organization of Indramayu centered on land ownership has historically shaped the structural subordination that persists to this day. To illustrate, in Karanglayung, which is inhabited by some 3000 people, half of the 350-hectares *hamparan* is owned by only eight individuals. Indramayu is characterized by a high proportion of non-landowning households that cannot make a living solely through agriculture as they can only rely on rice growing for short lengths of time. In 2013, the Central Statistics Agency (BPS) reported that there were 91,415 landless households and 162,455 small-scale, semi-subsistence farmer households in Indramayu (BPS 2013). Locals have long accustomed to hold seasonal off-farm jobs and adopt migration to other areas as a strategy of adjustment to economic difficulty.

The advent of the post-colonial state, and the developmental state that followed, exacerbates existing precarity as attempts to modernize the agricultural sector became counterproductive in the long run. In post-independence Indonesia, one of the first key priorities was to bring in robust infrastructure to support wet-rice cultivation, in particular irrigation. The building of the Jatiluhur dam, which began in the 1950s, marked an important milestone; however, the modernizing process became much more intensified following Soeharto's rise to power and concomitantly, the ascent of his technocratic state. Under the Government's development scheme, orientation to productivity became key. It is important to understand the political aspects of rice agriculture here. As the main staple food for most Indonesians, rice is not merely the main source of carbohydrates, it holds symbolic value as well. At his first annual state address in 1967, Soeharto emphasized the central role of rice in ensuring political stability. *Swasembada*, or self-sufficiency was the administrative main goal, and his priority during the first REPELITA was to launch programs such as "mass guidance" (*Bimbingan Massal—Bimas*) and "mass instruction" (*Instruksi Massal—Inmas*), which were meant to modernize agricultural practices and help farmers implement new technologies and high-productive yields rice varieties developed in the neighboring Southeast Asian countries of Philippines, Thailand, and Malaysia. With the Green Revolution, the New Order period then saw immense administering of state-approved agricultural input; seeds, fertilizers, and pesticides.

There are two consequences of high-input agriculture. Firstly, rice-growing became dependent on non-renewable input, which leads to small-scale farming turning it into a non-profitable business since higher input means higher production cost. Although the government officially subsidizes certain components such as fertilizers, in practice, distribution often does not reach all farmers. Additionally, fertilizer companies and pesticide producers carry out aggressive promotion, capitalizing on ecological vulnerability to scare farmers. Our ethnographic engagement with Indramayu farmers since 2006 reveals how they apply pesticides without really understanding its purpose. This excessive use of pesticides ("pesticides addiction," as the farmers call it) leads to a culmination of problems beyond economic terms such as health and environmental ones. The first sign of the failure of the state's high-input agriculture occurred as early as 1986 when brown plant hoppers (*hama wereng*) wreak havoc across rice fields of Java. Cycles of pest outbreak continue to this day, the latest major one occurring in July–August 2017. In the end, the Green Revolution brought about unintended consequences as the introduction of agricultural technology and high-input cultivation by the state eventually led to the sector becoming inflexible and, at the same time, vulnerable. In Indramayu, agriculture has turned into a risky and low-income sector for landless/small-scale farmers. They use the metaphor of gambling to describe rice-farming, claiming that "We never know if we will get a good harvest or not."

Interlocutors generally contend that rice-growing is only profitable when a farmer has access to at least 3–5 *bahu* (*bahu* = 7000 square meters). To illustrate, interlocutor Pak Ibrahim rents 1 *bahu* per growing season for

Rp. 15 million, which yields a harvest of 5–6 tons and generates around a total of Rp. 22.5 million of income. If the cost of production is set at Rp. 5 million, this means that his profit is only Rp. 2.5 million for the entire season. This calculation does not take into account a pest-outbreak scenario, which can result in productivity dropping to 1 ton/*bahu*. Farmers estimate that they need at least one *bahu* of extra investment alone to absorb potential loss. In such debt-prone setting, Indramayu farmers always look to generate fast cash. Farmers moonlight in every way possible. Studies of Indramayu have converged on identifying three main categories of livelihood strategies, namely agriculture, non-farming activities, and migration (see, for example, Abdurrahim et al. 2014). Migration presents a real livelihood option, especially when considering the other alternatives. Analysts have highlighted locals' readiness to embrace occupation in the sex industry and the long-standing widely accepted "cultural tradition" of sending teens and young women (Sudrajat 2005, 767; Mulyani 2007, 45; ILO-IPEC 1998, 91—all as quoted in Sano 2012), thus rendering Indramayu a particularly precarious site for women.

Today, Indramayu is firmly established as one of the main migrant source areas in Indonesia. Official statistics from the BNP2TKI show that over the years, it is consistently among Indonesia's top two migrant-sending areas (see Table 2.1). The rise of migration as a livelihood also creates opportunities for another livelihood for *non*-migrants, i.e., recruiting.

Brokers in Indramayu: Legal, Occupational and Economic Precarity

It is important to stress that migrant recruiters are not the only brokers operating in Indramayu. Brokerage also flourishes for other areas, most importantly prostitution. Sano (2012) mentions how the sex trade is something of an open secret in Indramayu and that the region is an important recruiting ground for sex workers. This lends a stigma of illicitness to brokerage, which also impacted our research in a significant way, most notably in terms of interlocutors' willingness to participate. In recent times, there has been considerable scrutiny from media and NGOs in terms of this. Throughout fieldwork, interlocutors expressed their concerns, "I'm afraid. You might turn out to be a journalist." Making specific allusion to risk, interlocutor Pak Mumun saw his position as particularly vulnerable due to increased scrutiny from non-state actors, "We take great *risks*. The NGOs and journalists, they monitor us, if we make mistakes, we're done

Table 2.1 Top 10 migrant sending areas in Indonesia (annual placement data)

Region (Town/Regency)	2011	2012	2013	2014	2015	2016	2017 (up to February)
East Lombok	28,391	19,936	33,287	29,510	25,772	19,274	2,267
Indramayu	33,213	28,949	28,410	25,521	19,025	16,625	2,261
Cilacap	22,133	19,799	17,592	16,013	10,753	9,574	1,209
Cirebon (Regency)	19,152	16,755	18,675	15,786	10,953	10,078	1,376
Central Lombok	23,352	13,675	14,793	14,109	12,175	10,907	1,413
Cianjur	18,386	12,266	14,639	11,311	5,437	3,227	N/A
Kendal	13,977	10,967	11.497	11,212	7,581	6,391	772
Ponorogo	11,539	10,940	10,494	8,869	6,443	6,597	747
Subang	11,918	9,742	10,661	8,357	7,254	6,522	953
Brebes	13,742	11,291	9,336	8,216	5,292	4,310	633

(*Source* BNP2TKI [2016a, b])

for… When a problem arises, even if it's just a small one, they really make a fuss."

Illegal activities are indeed mainly associated with brokers despite the problematic and widely known public–private partnership in Indonesia's labor outmigration. While the government is often a target of criticisms, it is called upon as protector of migrants (Rudnyckyj 2004; Silvey 2004). In recent years, the government has even announced it would undertake more efforts to put an end to brokering practices. Current Head of BNP2TKI, Nusron Wahid, has repeatedly touted eliminating illegal brokerage is one of main measures to prevent recruitment of undocumented migrants ("non-procedural TKI").[2]

Denigration against brokers rarely seems to come from the general population though. The prevalence of brokers in Indramayu is evident, as well as locals' knowledge of their activities. Informal conversations with locals

---

[2] Wahid boldly proclaimed brokerage as the reason behind lofty recruitment fees. However, till date, the BNP2TKI has not really provided a solution to this problem. Instead, the Coordinating Agency has proposed action that seems to be ineffectual, contradicting each other and not acknowledging the root causes of brokerage. See BNP2TKI (2014) and *Kompas* (2015).

reveal both cognizance of the reality of migration and familiarity with intermediating practices. For instance, when one of the members of the research team casually asked if our farmer interlocutors knew of any brokers in their village, their immediate response was: "Who is the candidate? Is the person who wants to work abroad male or female?" Indeed, one interlocutor asserted that "Once the community hears of someone expressing interest in migrating, more than one sponsor will immediately approach us. Not just one person, but five at once!"

In general, locals differentiate brokers into two types—full-time or part-time. Full-time brokers are those whose main source of income is the recruitment of migrant workers, whereas part-time brokers partake in recruitment as an alternative among other off-farming jobs. Part-time brokerage is often practiced by small-scale farmers (rice-farming or livestock farming). Typically, they have access to or own a small plot of agricultural land. The main difference between full-time and part-time brokers lies in how the latter rely mostly on friendship and familial relations in their recruitment activities. Not rarely do they migrate their own family members or relatives. Oftentimes, full-time brokers are stationary who wait for potential clients to come to them. In contrast, part-timers actively scout for clients: "*Kerjaannya keliling-keliling desa cari TKI.*" [They spend their day touring around the village to scout for recruits.] Owing to the mobile nature of their scouting, part-time brokers are customarily known as "petugas lapangan" (PL) or field agents, who in turn hand over recruits to full-time brokers who function as sponsors and often started out as field agents themselves. Sponsors and PL commonly work out deals between them regarding the sharing of profit they get from each recruit. Hajjah Ina, a sponsor, remarked that she had to employ a lot of field agents, acknowledging the need to enlist PL to tap deep into supply of workers.

The second source of Indramayu brokers' anxiety is risks that stem from the job itself. Pak Dayat remarked that there was nothing enjoyable about his sponsoring job. His partner, Pak Yadi, agreed, "We don't sleep well." Illustrating his point, Pak Yadi delineated his situation with a current recruit, who still had not been cleared for placement despite having spent three months at a training center. Another recruit weighing his mind was a young woman who had departed abroad three months earlier but from whom no news had arrived. He felt considerable pressure in both cases as he was subjected to inquiries from both families. "I'm the one who has to deal with all the questions." His statement confirms Spaan's (1994) observation that due to the level in which they operate, rural brokers carry the risk of recruitment as they have a reputation to maintain. Occupational risk further reveals the relationship between recruitment agencies and informal brokers, which is deeply asymmetrical. According to Pak Dadang, brokers' intermediation is "good for the company," as it simultaneously hides them from view, and provides a human face for brokerage. The point, he said, is that "someone has to be held accountable."

Lastly, precarity as informality itself is an aspect that must not be overlooked. While they are indispensable to recruitment agencies, most brokers (especially field agents) do not have formal contracts with agencies they supply workers to. Pak Mumun took on the metaphor of war to describe his position relative to the agencies: "If we were in a battlefield, for sure it's us who'd die first. The PPTKIS, they have a lot of money, they can hire lawyers. Whereas for us? Who, what can we rely on, should any problem arises?"

Brokerage as an Accepted Livelihood

In the next two sections, we consider more closely why brokering continues despite commonplace vilification of informal brokers. Interlocutors frequently referred to the metaphor of a bridge here. This is well-elaborated on by Lindquist who suggests that "the dual process of centralization of migration control and fragmentation of labour recruitment has created a space of mediation for individuals who can navigate bureaucratic process while embodying the ethical qualities that convince Indonesian villagers to become migrants" (2012, 69). Our research findings corroborate with this. One prominent feature of Indonesia's labor outmigration is the institutional gap; the industry flourishes but not the institutions that protect workers. The public sector has been slow in its involvement in Indonesia's labor outmigration. Despite deployment of migrant workers since the late 1960s, for a long time, Indonesia did not have a national legal framework stipulating the principles of its migration policies, especially concerning the protection of rights and provision of needs of migrant workers. The Law No. 39/2004 on the Placement and Protection of Indonesian Workers Abroad only came about six years after *Reformasi*. In the post-1998 era, given this context of lagging institutionalization, migrant workers cannot rely on state; the locus of trust is thus on the brokers.

While this discussion of trust is important, a focus on income generation allows for more productive explorations concerning the perpetuation of brokerage activities. We propose to expand on two points, based on the comments from a key interlocutor, Pak Dadang. Reflecting on why brokering practices persist, he offered the following answer.

> Why the company must use sponsors? It is common in Indramayu to use them, if not, where would the sponsors go? It's their job, right? Would the government take responsibility if the sponsors become unemployed? … The key point remains that they are also looking to eat.

Previous analyses have meticulously documented the shifting landscape from undocumented to documented migration. They reaffirm the impression of the continuation of Indonesian labor outmigration as in essence *an industry*. That the involvement of mediation practices characterizes each distinct migration era also means that someone always seeks to generate income from the migration process. Most brokers we gathered data on considered "mediation" as one among the many jobs they were involved in. The Indonesian word *serabutan* which roughly translates as "odd jobs" is commonly used to describe the various income-generating activities that they perform. Regularly employment has no place where precarity is the norm. Instead, *halal* is often used as the benchmark. In Indonesia, where the state is often "absent" and pious democracy is on the ascend, the involvement in "illegal" activities poses less of a problem as long as it does not go against the tenets of religion. Indeed, it should be noted that many female ex-migrant brokers of prominent stature in Indramayu use the respectable religious designation of *hajjah*. Below is a direct quote from Pak Mumun,

> Other activities, *serabutan*… well, you know, odd jobs, what's important is that it's a *halal*. Working in *sawah*, I can do that, no problem, I can drive *becak* (rickshaw). There is no standard, I can do anything, as long as it's *halal*.

Highlighting how agriculture remains a core activity, brokers mainly report rice-growing or farming-related activities as their main occupation. Pak Dayat's main job, for example, is breeding birds, which Pak Yadi, his friend and another broker, described as an example of "typical business for people of our class status." Meanwhile, Pak Hamid simply pointed to brokering as a naturally available job for a *kampung* person as himself. "What do you expect? People like us cannot possibly work in an office." While these remarks affirm the agricultural sector's iconic status in Indramayu, we acknowledge that as the district becomes more urbanized, more livelihoods not related to farming open up, especially in bazaar towns like Jatibarang. For many brokers, brokering is at best "a-good-enough-for-now" source of income. Pak Yadi remarked that "For sure, we'll quit being sponsors, if we have a steady job."

Pak Dadang's eloquence betrayed his level of education.

> Me? My background, I do pond farming *(petani tambak)*, although I am off from that currently, I do that (only) sometimes (anyhow), I'm *nggak jelas* (obscure), it's complicated for me... I have a degree in Forestry, S. Hut., I graduated from Jatinangor. My major was in agriculture.

Jatinangor here refers to the location of Universitas Padjadjaran, one of the best universities in Indonesia. His dream was to secure a profession as an agricultural counselor with the Ministry of Agriculture. "But you know how it is to work in the government, I have a university degree, but until now, I still can't get certified... so I simply chose to be a farmer." Pak Dadang's predicament accentuates the general situation in Indramayu, where prospect for employment is limited. Indramayu's Regional Office of Manpower and Transmigration Department recorded that in 2015, there were as many as 35,940 job seekers unable to find work placement in the district. Indeed, high unemployment greatly contributes, if not conditions, the wide acceptance of brokering as a livelihood. Pak Dadang's underlying statement, "they are looking to eat," reflects overall permissiveness toward brokering in the absence of other employment options. Even official statements from the government to regulate or banish brokers altogether seem more about appearances as everybody is aware of their shortcomings in job creation.

INTIMACY AND THE MIGRATION MARKET

A second important insight is further hinted in Pak Dadang's subsequent assertion:

> Indonesia is unlike other countries, for example, let's consider how people in other countries behave when they are seeking entertainment... for instance, if they want to go to the night market, they have to go out (to the bazaar), but here in Indonesia, there is no need for that. The night market comes to you (the hawkers, the bazaar), the service providers come to you... they enter the alleys.

This commentary alludes to the deep entanglement of the personal in recruitment practices and immediately reminds of the opening ethnographic scene with Euis at the PPTKIS. The border between migrant and broker is porous and thin. Complementing Lindquist's analysis on the personal which he discussed through the notion of trust, we dissect it through observations of the following: the route to brokering, the downplaying of recruitment activities, and the idea of recruiting as a noble act.

Broker interlocutors' delineation of their route to the mediating business is particularly telling of locals' intimate entanglement with Indramayu's migration industry. Most report starting out in the business through personal experience. This can take the form of being initiated to the industry by relatives, such as Pak Mumun, who first learned by observing his uncle and friends. "I paid attention... listened." He learned to hang around with the agency staff, assessing which agencies are good (the ones offering higher remuneration) and which destinations are more lucrative.

Other brokers started by migrating relatives like Pak Yadi who "migrated" his own wife, after their initial experience being swindled by middlemen during her recruitment process. "At first, we kept on being duped by the brokers. Finally, we decided to go the agency ourselves; we looked up the agency and found the office. Eventually, the staff told me that I should just work there." Pak Yadi hints at how the transition to brokering often occurs very subtly. Again, with Euis in mind, "This is how it happens oft-times, a person comes to an agency (to accompany) a relative... she takes the recruit there or visits them at the training center, before she knows it, once she's on her way home, she has already become a sponsor."

The act of migrating relatives and close friends leads to the tendency of some of the brokers to downplay their recruiting activities. They usually refer to brokering not as a real job. They would insist that they were instead, "merely helping." However, it is unclear whether the "recruiting as helping" narrative should be read as an expression of guilt. Another interlocutor, Supraja, relayed a more complex motive. A former village head who took pride in Indramayu's fame as a mango-producing town, he felt shame for Indramayu being more renowned for supplying prostitutes to big cities such as Jakarta. "There was open recruitment for jobs in the Middle East at the time, and so we encouraged those unemployed to go to the Middle East to support their family, and to straighten Indramayu's (reputation) so it's no longer known mainly for its commercial sex workers."

Maintaining brokering activities as helping also serves to accentuate brokers' continuing precarity. Pak Mumun insisted that his primary intention was as follows:

> Not to accumulate wealth. There's no such thing as rich sponsors... it's a lie. Sponsors lead difficult lives. None of us is rich, unless they come from a privileged background... Me, I am struggling.

Indeed, brokering—like migration—does not guarantee a sure way out of poverty. After 17 years of brokering, Pak Mumum still lives with his parents. The house he lives in is old and dilapidated; the wall paints are fading; the wooden railings have been eaten away by termites. He lamented: "If I see someone who I recruited become successful, then praise be to Allah. Of course, it's due to their own hard work, they're the ones who work abroad, not me. *Alhamdulillah*... But I am the one who remains like this..."

Brokers who were former migrants themselves generally spoke from intimate personal experiences. Pak Dadang's extensive knowledge of the migration industry clearly draws upon his previous overseas employment includes stints in Japan, Singapore, Johor Bahru, and South Korea, as well as working as part of a ship's crew in Australia. Regarding this particular group of recruiters, a final aspect that we would like to expand on is the prominence of female recruiters in Indramayu, i.e., feminization of migration from the vantage point of brokerage.

Feminization of Migration Brokerage

Hj. Inayah has been involved in migration brokerage since 2007. A former migrant worker, she used to work in Saudi Arabia. The first time she went was in 1986. She worked in Jeddah for 3.5 years, followed by a second term of employment in Mecca between 1994 and 1997. The story she narrated of how she first became initiated into brokering closely mirrors the previous scene with Euis. When Hj. Inayah sought to be deployed for the third time, the agency informed her that she had reached the age limit and was thus no longer qualified to go. She describes her trajectory as follows:

> I also suffer from high blood pressure, so I was no longer a fit candidate. I couldn't go, but they told me. If you are interested, you can find people who want to work abroad instead. At the time, I didn't know how, how to talk to people, it was a slow process, I didn't suddenly become a sponsor, at

first, I just tried talking to my friend. The first time I sponsored, I only got Rp. 50,000,-. I was just helping out a friend.

Hajjah Inayah started out as a field agent, "I initially brought just one or two persons, at the time I liaised with someone 'inside,' I recruited on behalf of someone else, now I go directly to the agency." Hajjah Inayah spoke of her past frustrations working as a field agent. At times, she had agreed to hand out some advance money for her recruits, but the sponsor withheld it, not enabling her to keep her promise to the candidate and thus jeopardized the process. Eventually, she decided to take matters into her own hands by becoming a sponsor, rather than "working for someone else." Things are different now from when she started out. She now employs field agents dispersed between Indramayu and Cirebon. "The first year or two, I used to go around (to find candidates), now I don't. Now, the recruits come to me. They know my number; I just wait for the phone call."

Here, we found that women are more likely to succeed in migration brokerage than men. They are more likely to make a "profession" as recruiters, while men tend to see brokerage just as another variegated short-term occupation employed to generate fast cash. Whether female former migrant workers more successful brokering career owes more to their capitalizing on their experience—i.e., the worldview they obtained through their own migration serves as a source of moral authority—or men's disposition to regard intermediation more pragmatically is a point that warrants further consideration.

Conclusion

In this chapter, we presented a view of the migration industry from the vantage point of Indramayu, an important source of migrants in Indonesia. If the *sawah*, which is open to all kinds of participation through its labor-intensive nature, serves as a metaphor for a culture of "shared poverty," migration presents an enterprise for the precariat to carve out livelihoods. Migration generates multiple venues for income generation—if one does not migrate, one can migrate others. In our Southern reading of the precarity of Indramayu as a site, we seek to eschew seeing brokers as invariably unscrupulous. This is not to deny the real likelihood of exploitation of migrant workers amid brokering practices, but to contend that viewing brokering practices through a lens of precarity allows for a more complete moral economic understanding. We also note that the experiences of Indramayu's growing rural precariat, of which the brokers are a part, present themselves differently from their Northern counterparts; and it remains to be seen whether they can be viewed as the new dangerous class, which Standing (2011) envisages will bring about social transformation.

Brokering is an option out of many available amid the existing neoliberal (re-)structuring of an agrarian society in transition. In Indramayu, like migration, brokering has become a commonplace and acceptable household response to the precarity brought upon by the state's development strategies. In diversifying livelihoods, households not only have the option to have family members migrate abroad, but also to involve themselves in brokerage. Situating our work in the broader studies of migration and the context of agricultural transition, we see this study as making an important contribution to expanding our thinking of migration by also taking the ecological dimension into account. Recent works stimulating discussion in this direction include Peluso and Purwanto's (2018) study, which looks at how labor migration alters land use, including forest landscapes. Our approach differs in how, through focus on the migration industry instead of remittances, we aim to avoid *ad interim* neoliberal optimism concerning migration and development.

Acknowledgements Our work would not be possible without our Dermayon interlocutors' generosity with their time, trust, and cultural knowledge of the world they live in. The authors would like to thank Johan Lindquist for his close reading of an earlier version of this chapter and supportive feedback, as well as well as participants of the workshop "The Migration Industry: Facilitators and Brokerage in Asia," organized by the Asia Research Institute, National University of Singapore, on June 1–2, 2017, for their thought-provoking comments. This research did not receive any specific grant from funding agencies, whether public, commercial, or non-profit.

References

Abdurrahim, A. Y., Dharmawan, A. H., Sunito, S., & Sudiana, I. M. (2014). Kerentanan ekologi dan strategi penghidupan pertanian masyarakat desa persawahan tadah hujan di Pantura, Indramayu. *Jurnal Kependudukan Indonesia, 9*(1), 25–44.

BPS. (2013). *Sensus Pertanian 2013 Provinsi Jawa Barat: Jumlah Rumah Tangga Usaha Pertanian Pengguna Lahan dan Rumah Tangga Petani Gurem menurut Wilayah Tahun 2003 dan 2013*. Accessed August 5, 2019. https://st2013.bps.go.id/dev2/index.php/site/tabel?tid=22&wid=3200000000.

Castles, S. (2015). Migration, precarious work, and rights: Historical and current perspectives. In C. U. Schierup, R. Munck, B. Likic-Brobric, & A. Neergaard (Eds.), *Migration, precarity, and global governance: Challenges and opportunities for labour* (pp. 46–67). Oxford: Oxford University Press.

Castles, S., de Haas, H., & Miller, M. J. (2013). *The age of migration: International population movements in the modern world*. New York: Palgrave Macmillan.

Cranston, S., Schapedonk, J., & Spaan, E. (2018). New directions in exploring the migration industries: Introduction to special issue. *Journal of Ethnic and Migration Studies, 44*(4), 543–557.

Deshingkar, P. (2018). The making and unmaking of precarious, ideal subjects—Migration brokerage in the Global South. *Journal of Ethnic and Migration Studies*. https://doi.org/10.1080/1369183x.2018.1528094.

Delgado-Wise, R. (2015). Migration and labour under neoliberal globalization. In C. U. Schierup, R. Munck, B. Likic-Brobric, & A. Neergaard (Eds.), *Migration, precarity, and global governance: Challenges and opportunities for labour* (pp. 25–45). Oxford: Oxford University Press.

Hansen, G. E. (1972). Indonesia's green revolution: The abandonment of a non-market strategy toward change. *Asian Survey, 12*(11), 932–946.

Hugo, G. (2000a). The impact of the crisis on internal population movement in Indonesia. *Bulletin of Indonesian Economic Studies, 36*(2), 115–138.

Hugo, G. (2000b). The crisis and international population movement in Indonesia. *Asian and Pacific Migration Journal, 9*(1), 93.

Kalleberg, A. L., & Hewison, K. (2013). Precarious work and the challenge for Asia. *American Behavioral Scientist, 57*(3), 271–288.

Kompas. (2015, October 16). BNP2TKI Kejar Calo dan Sponsor TKI Illegal.

Lee, C. K., & Kofman, Y. (2012). The politics of precarity: Views beyond the United States. *Work and Occupations, 39*(4), 388–408.

Li, T. M. (2010). To make live or let die? Rural dispossession and the protection of surplus populations. *Antipode, 41*(1), 66–93.

Lindquist, J. (2010). Labour recruitment, circuits of capital and gendered mobility: Reconceptualizing the Indonesian migration industry. *Pacific Affairs, 83*(1), 115–132.

Lindquist, J. (2012). The elementary school teacher, the thug and his grandmother: Informal brokers and transnational migration from Indonesia. *Pacific Affairs, 85*(1), 69–89.

Márquez, H., & Delgado Wise, R. (2011). A Southern perspective on forced migration and alternative development. *Migración Y Desarrollo, 9*(16), 3–42.

Munck, R. (2013). The precariat: A view from the South. *Third World Quarterly*, *34*(5), 747–762.
Neilson, B., & Rossiter, N. (2008). Precarity as a political concept, or, fordism as exception. *Theory, Culture & Society*, *25*(7–8), 51–72.
Paret, M., & Gleeson, S. (2016). Precarity and agency through a migration lens. *Citizenship Studies*, *20*(3–4), 277–294.
Peluso, N. L., & Purwanto, A. B. (2018). The remittance forest: Turning mobile labor into agrarian capital. *Singapore Journal of Tropical Geography*, *39*(1), 6–36.
Rudnyckyj, D. (2004). Technologies of servitude: Governmentality and Indonesian transnational labor migration. *Anthropological Quarterly*, *77*(3), 407–434.
Sano, A. (2012). Agency and resilience in the sex trade: Adolescent girls in rural Indramayu. *Asia Pacific Journal of Anthropology*, *13*(1), 21–35.
Scott, J. (2009). *The art of not being governed: An anarchist history of upland Southeast Asia*. New Haven: Yale University Press.
Silvey, R. (2004). Transnational domestication: State power and Indonesian migrant women in Saudi Arabia. *Political Geography*, *23*(3), 245–264.
Sørensen, N. N. (2012). Revisiting the migration-development nexus: From social networks and remittances to markets for migration control. *International Migration*, *50*(3), 61–76.
Spaan, E. (1994). Taikongs and calos: The role of middlemen and brokers in Javanese international migration. *International Migration Review*, *28*(1), 93–113.
Standing, G. (2011). *The precariat: A new dangerous class*. London and New York: Bloomsbury.
Standing, G. (2015). From denizens to citizens: Forging a precariat charter. In C. U. Schierup, R. Munck, B. Likic-Brobric, & A. Neergaard (Eds.), *Migration, precarity, and global governance: Challenges and opportunities for labour* (pp. 83–100). Oxford: Oxford University Press.
Vosko, L. F. (2010). *Managing the margins: Gender, citizenship, and the international regulation of precarious employment*. New York: Oxford University Press.

Government Documents

BNP2TKI. (2014, December 10). *Kepala BNP2TKI: Berantas Calo TKI, Aktifkan BLKLN dan Berdayakan TKI Purna*. Accessed April 23, 2017. http://www.bnp2tki.go.id/read/9663/Kepala-BNP2TKI-:-Berantas-Calo-TKI-Aktifkan-BLKLN-dan-Berdayakan-TKI-Purna/.
BPS Indramayu. (2016). *Kabupaten Indramayu dalam Angka*. Accessed April 23, 2017. https://indramayukab.bps.go.id/new/website/pdf_publikasi/Kabupaten-Indramayu-Dalam-Angka-2016.pdf.
Pusat Penelitian dan Pengembangan Informasi BNP2TKI. (2016a). *Data Penempatan dan Perlindungan Tenaga Kerja Indonesia Tahun 2016*. Accessed

April 11, 2017. http://www.bnp2tki.go.id/uploads/data/data_08-02-2017_111324_Data-P2TKI_tahun_2016.pdf.

Pusat Penelitian dan Pengembangan Informasi BNP2TKI. (2016b). *Data Penempatan TKI Tahun 2017 (s.d. Februari)*. Accessed April 11, 2017. http://www.bnp2tki.go.id/uploads/data/data_10-03-2017_092059_Laporan_Pengolahan_Data_BNP2TKI_2017_(FEBRUARI)_1.pdf.

CHAPTER 3

Brokered (Il)legality: Co-producing the Status of Migrants from Myanmar to Thailand

Indrė Balčaitė

Introduction

Originally from Kayin State, Myanmar (Burma),[1] Naw Eh Moo has been working in Thailand since 2004. The first time she went with a friend of hers who had worked in Bangkok before. They hired a broker to travel from Hpa-an (Pa-an) in Kayin State to Central Thailand, undocumented. Within two years of her arrival in Bangkok, Naw Eh Moo registered as a migrant worker with her employer's help. 'Legalisation' meant that she had to confirm her address at an immigration centre every 90 days. Unwilling to hire a broker who would do it for her or pay a day's wage to the immigration officer to jump the queue, she waited from 5 a.m. till 2 p.m. to

---

[1] As the official name of the country was changed in 1989, I use 'Burma' in the period before and 'Myanmar' thereafter. I adopt other changed place names but add the previous form in parentheses at first mention. However, I call the ethnic minority in focus 'Karen' rather than 'Kayin'.

I. Balčaitė (✉)
London, UK

© The Author(s) 2020
M. Baas (ed.), *The Migration Industry in Asia*,
https://doi.org/10.1007/978-981-13-9694-6_3

get the necessary stamp. When the opportunity presented itself in 2009, Naw Eh Moo underwent 'nationality verification'—a process mediated by agencies—and was issued a temporary Myanmar passport with a Thai visa. Having a passport enabled her to visit her village in Myanmar every year but each time she still had to obtain a re-entry permit from the local immigration centre before travelling. This meant queuing, paying extra or hiring a broker again. By December 2015, her temporary passport had expired and there was no information on how migrants could retain their legal status if at all. Naw Eh Moo and her husband went back to Myanmar and applied to join the official labour import scheme based on the intergovernmental Myanmar–Thailand Memorandum of Understanding (MoU). They paid a broker who warned them that it would be a multi-stage process. Two months later, Naw Eh Moo and her husband still had no news and their employer in Thailand was growing impatient. Hence, the couple paid another broker to be smuggled into Thailand in March 2016. After a few months, they registered as migrant workers, obtaining 'pink cards' again.

Based on three interviews with Naw Eh Moo in 2013 and 2016, the summary above sheds light on the omnipresence of brokerage in migration from Myanmar to Thailand. Whether documented or undocumented, low-paid migration is heavily brokered and expensive and results in legal precarity. The method of arrival and the migrants' legal status at the time do not determine the conditions that they end up in. In fact, the social networks available to the migrants-to-be are more indicative of whether they will join the intergovernmental guestwork scheme or set off as undocumented migrants. Either way, they enlist individual brokers collaborating with state agents on both sides of the border. In the former case, brokers work with a cumbersome multi-layered bureaucracy in both countries following lengthy procedures. In the latter, they rely on certain individuals within those bureaucracies to bypass the procedures for quick results. From the point of the Karen migrants, brokerage is unavoidable so they prefer the fast, though undocumented travel with lower upfront costs and fewer restrictions. Their concern is not the choice between a brokered and unbrokered entry but between a 'good' and a 'bad' broker. The entry—as well as departure—is brokered anyway as the state, brokers and migrants co-produce their status.

Migrants' choices are reflective of the migration infrastructure that has emerged to shape the Myanmar–Thailand migration flow since the 1990s. In the current constellation of the migration regime, brokers, fixers and mediators are indispensable to migrants as they are to the agents of the state due to regulations and its implementation. Brokerage services available cover the spectrum of (il)legality, ranging from licensed agencies operating officially and legally to unregulated and informal actors as well as human smugglers. This spectrum of brokerage blurs the boundary between the state and the market.

In this article, I rely on fourteen months of fieldwork conducted in Myanmar and Thailand between 2012 and 2016.[2] With the help of co-researchers, I conducted in-depth semi-structured interviews with around 90 migrants from Myanmar to Thailand as well as other, less formal exchanges. Most of the interlocutors self-identified as Karen and came from a village in Hpa-an Township, Kayin State, Myanmar. Those who were migrants at the time of the interview were mostly working in Greater Bangkok. The majority of research participants had arrived in Thailand undocumented. Only two were MoU workers but the findings from their interviews are well-supported by other research (International Labour Organization 2015; Hall 2012) and conversations with several Burmese migrant labour activists in Thailand. I also talked to one former MoU facilitator, one former and one active human smuggler. Most names used in the article are pseudonyms.

The paper consists of three parts. In the first, I briefly lay out the theoretical framework of my approach to brokerage and situate it in relation to my empirical material. Secondly, I discuss the 'legal' and 'illegal' methods of low-paid labour migration from Myanmar to Thailand, demonstrating that the supposedly safer channel is not attractive due to complicated processes, financial and time costs and the lack of freedom. In the third part, I turn to practicalities of living as a low-paid migrant in Thailand. The possibility to 'legalise' after arrival also partly explains why the 'legal' migrant labour recruitment scheme is relatively unpopular. Moreover, the 'legalisation' industry illustrates that 'legal' and 'illegal' channels of arrival blur into each other as part of the same migration management system. The process of regularising one's status and sustaining it is also tangled in brokerage networks.

---

[2] Partly funded by SOAS Additional Fieldwork Grant, SOAS Centre for South-East Asian Studies Small Grant and Santander Mobility Grant.

Brokerage as Central to Migration

The prevailing image of a desirable migrant is that of a law-abiding independent individual travelling through the authorised channels after obtaining the required documentation. McKeown (2012; 2008, 66–89) dates the rise of this image back to the early twentieth century when intensifying state regulation of migration banished migration mediators to the margins. The tightening of border controls—a worldwide trend ever since—aimed specifically at sifting through migration flows to separate 'free migrants' from 'broker's prey' (McKeown 2012, 22–23).[3] The current policy preoccupation with human smuggling and trafficking as organised crime proves the long-lasting appeal of this distinction.

The focus on the agency of migrants themselves has not only glossed over the involvement of brokers but also obscured the impact of state regulations on migration (McKeown 2012, 24). Lindquist et al. (2012, 9) have suggested redirecting the gaze of migration scholars to the 'black box' of migration infrastructure—institutions, networks and people moving migrants from one place to another. Xiang and Lindquist (2014, S124, S142) define infrastructure as 'a multi-faceted middle space of mediation' where commercial recruitment intermediaries, bureaucrats, technologies, NGOs and migrants networks interact (see also Lin et al. 2017). Cranston et al. (2017) label this phenomenon 'migration industry', expanding the term's interpretation beyond its commercial implications (see Hernández-León 2013, 25; Xiang and Lindquist 2014, S133; Salt and Stein 1997). In this paper, commercial aspects are important but migration merchants offer more than paid migration services alone. In the words of Alpes (2013, 9–12; 2017, 59–64), brokers trade in transformative potentials, e.g. the possibility of improving one's status as a result of migration. In recognition, I use the terms 'migration infrastructure' and 'migration industry' interchangeably.

Across Asia, both migration regulation and migrant numbers have grown since the 1990s, leading to flourishing migration brokerage (Xiang and Lindquist 2014, S122–S123; Xiang 2012, 48). Asian countries are in denial about their dependence on immigration to fill low-paid jobs (Castles 2004; Castles et al. 2014, 170; Ananta and Arifin 2004, 24). As a result,

---

[3] See, for example, Alpes (2013, 4; 2017, 104) on how the foreign embassies in Cameroon discourage visa applicants from using mediators or Khosravi (2010, 27) on the 'animalisation' of human smugglers to demonstrate their vulnerability on the wrong side of the law.

time-restricted guestwork programmes ruling out residence and citizenship are on the rise. Hailed as 'safe' migration opportunities, they are just the other side of human trafficking (McKeown 2012, 43). As the article will demonstrate, guestwork and human trafficking can be similar 'migrant-exporting schemes' (Kyle and Siracusa 2005, 156). Sometimes, the single fact that they produce migrants on the opposite sides of the legal/illegal spectrum is what differentiates them. In guestwork programmes, the state acts as a migration broker for 'legal' migrant labour, whereas human smugglers and traffickers defy the official regulations to procure undocumented migrant workers. However, the outcomes of the two types of schemes can be hard to tell apart. As Lan (2007) argued about Filipina domestic workers in Taiwan, rigid regimes of regulation produce legality that is enslaving and illegality that is paradoxically empowering.

Although Xiang and Lindquist (2014, S125, f. 10) cite Myanmar as an extreme case of underdeveloped migration infrastructure, Myanmar–Thailand migration flow, the busiest within mainland Southeast Asia, conforms to pan-Asian trends. Despite severely restricting outmigration in theory, the Myanmar state did not actually control most of its border into the 1990s. A tightening border regime coincided with an ever-growing demand for labour migration especially after the Asian financial crisis, resulting in the proliferation of migration brokers arranging undocumented travel to Thailand and later also onwards to Malaysia. Until 1999, the Burmese government refused to acknowledge the presence of Burmese citizens in Thailand (Caouette et al. 2000, 47, n. 23). Only in the late 2000s did the neighbouring countries create a channel for 'legal' import of low-paid labour (MoU). Burmese migrant labour activists widely call this recruitment scheme 'legal trafficking'. Although it does offer 'legal' border crossing and time-restricted stay in Thailand, restraints attached to the scheme render this legality nominal: MoU migrants are more vulnerable to human and employment rights abuses than those arriving undocumented. In the eyes of the migrants (Kyle and Siracusa 2005), travel to Thailand in either case is brokered and costly and leads to precarious legal status.

To understand the complex migration industry as a whole rather than scrutinising its fragment taken out of context, the analytical concept of brokerage should be applied across the board rather than on just one side of the state-sanctioned legal/illegal division (cf. Kyle and Siracusa 2005, 156; Alpes 2017, 19). Brokers as well as state agents operate across it, and the broader definition allows to capture this multiplicity and to interrogate the boundaries of state and market ethnographically (see Alpes 2017,

19, 25). Brokers on both sides of the Myanmar–Thailand border can assist with crossing it 'legally' or 'illegally', with transferring to another status or just with avoiding queues at the local immigration centre. There are agents specialising in human smuggling, official MoU migrant labour procurement scheme, nationality verification and day-to-day reporting.[4] Even the official agencies rely on individual brokers or agents operating informally. Their activities constitute the 'middle space of mediation' blurring the legal/illegal boundary and the state-broker distinction. Spaan and Hillmann (2013, 65) even suggest that the blurring of legal/illegal and of control/facilitation function is characteristic of migration industry.

From the migrants' point of view, both the 'legal' and 'illegal' dimensions of the migration industry operate within the same profitable field involving the same actors and not able to guarantee safety and rights. Brokers and state agents collaborate in arranging and taxing both regular and irregular arrivals. The 'legal' and the 'illegal' coalesce and mingle with each other. Certain flows are deemed 'illicit' just because they lack the official sanction of the state rather than due to any other characteristics (van Schendel 2005, 156; van Schendel and Abraham 2005, 4). Yet an unofficial agreement allows them in nevertheless. (Il)legality is a process produced by law (De Genova 2002) and commodified at every turn (Spaan and Hillmann 2013, 75). Rather than being an entitlement of compliant ('good') low-paid migrants, legality is instead a resource appropriated in the migration process and traded to migrants for a premium, as Molland (2012) observed in Lao migration to Thailand. That explains why guest-work programmes across Asia are so costly (see, e.g., Surak 2017; Kern and Müller-Böker 2015; Xiang 2012). However, many Burmese borderlanders have a viable alternative of travelling undocumented, as the next section demonstrates.

'Legal Trafficking'

Undocumented migration is widespread among Burmese migrants to Thailand as is considered a much simpler, faster and even cheaper procedure than the official labour recruitment scheme in place. The price of an undocumented arrival may be almost half of what documented migrants pay for participation in the MoU track. Both legality and illegality are brokered and

---

[4] For the purposes of this paper, I exclude the transnational money transfer services undertaken by brokers.

costly but a high premium applies to legality and its maintenance. Moreover, for the past decade, informal migration brokerage among the Karen has focused only on getting migrants to their destination in Thailand (i.e. human smuggling), whereas the state-managed guestwork scheme continues to control migrants throughout their employment not unlike the human traffickers do.[5] In such a situation, the state-sanctioned programme sources its clients mostly from the inner regions of Myanmar where informal brokerage networks—much more popular overall—do not reach. Given that money is paid to the authorities for passage in either case, state agents profit from undocumented migration rather than being harmed by it. From the migrants' point of view, the only apparent victim of the violations of immigration rules is the fictitious sovereignty of the state (see Kyle and Siracusa 2005, 153, 161).

Until a decade ago, Thai law did not foresee any legal entry for migrant labourers. The first Alien Employment Act B.E. 2521 (1978) was amended to accommodate a 'legal' channel for temporary employment of foreigners in low-paid jobs only in 2008 (International Labour Organization 2015, 5; Sciortino and Punpuing 2009a, 40). Thailand's intergovernmental Memoranda of Understanding (MoU) with its labour-exporting neighbours—Cambodia, Laos and Myanmar—signed in 2002–2003 created the basis for that. The MoU process should allow to obtain the documents and sign the job contract before leaving Myanmar. Unlike undocumented migrants, MoU participants obtain a passport, Thai visa and work permit before starting employment in Thailand. With their paperwork in order and a job guaranteed to be waiting, their situation should be more secure than of that of the undocumented migrants who face police and employer harassment.

In reality, only migrants with no cross-border networks of their own use the scheme as it is costly, time-consuming and restrictive (see also Natali et al. 2014, 19; International Labour Organization 2015, 13). The Thailand-Myanmar MoU process has been in operation since 2009. Close to 142,000 Burmese migrants had used it by November 2014 (International Labour Organization 2015, 6). In comparison, over 778,000 or 5.5 times more Burmese migrants had instead completed the National-

---

[5] Human smuggling and trafficking are punishable under the protocols to the UN Organized Crime Convention (United Nations 2000). Whereas human smuggling is considered to entail only securing the illegal passage into the country of work, human trafficking also encompasses coercive exploitation of the person's labour there (Ditmore and Wijers 2003, 80).

ity Verification scheme for regularising irregular migrants by July 2013 (Huguet 2014, 3).[6] A former MoU agent in Myanmar and a Burmese migrant labour activist in Thailand both told me that it was mostly people from central Myanmar (e.g. Yangon and Bago Regions) who were using the MoU process. U Myo and U Thant, two Bamar MoU construction workers from Bago and Irrawaddy Regions whom we interviewed in Bangkok, confirmed that many people from their rural communities migrated to work in Thailand through the MoU. U Myo and U Thant's friends gave them the phone number of an MoU agent working in Myawaddy. Meanwhile, those hailing from the eastern borderlands (Kayin, Mon, Shan States) had established their ethnic networks to the job market in Thailand (Arnold 2005, 290) before the MoU scheme started.

Participation in the MoU process is expensive. The official fees due before departure amount to 100,000 Myanmar kyat (MMK, around 74 USD in 2017–2018 exchange rates[7]) but 10,000 Thai baht (THB, 294 USD) are also deducted from the worker's salary in Thailand. Burmese migrant labour activists in Thailand—representatives of the Migrant Worker Rights Network based in Samut Sakhon interviewed in June 2013 and members of the umbrella forum Myanmar Migrant Network Bangkok in a meeting I attended in October 2016—contested that the actual costs of the programme rise to 200,000–400,000 MMK (147–294 USD) or more on the Burmese side and Thai employers demand 12,000–15,000 THB (353–441 USD) from the new arrivals. Hall (2012, 6) reports that early Burmese MoU workers arriving via the Kawthaung–Ranong border pass were spending even 650–1100 USD in total. U Myo and U Thant mentioned paying 200,000 MMK in 2013. They also travelled from Central Myanmar to Myawaddy on the border with Thailand at their own expense. After their passports expired, Naw Eh Moo and her husband (see above) paid over 400,000 MMK each to a broker in early 2017 to participate in the MoU scheme. In a country where the minimum wage is only 95.44 USD a month (National Wages and Productivity Commission 2019), these are considerable amounts of money. Many participants buy transformative potentials or hopes of a better income by getting into debt.

---

[6] The total number of Burmese migrant workers in Thailand is estimated to be up to 3 million. See, e.g., Ma (2017).

[7] Here and elsewhere, the calculations are based on Trading Economics (2018a, b) data.

The implementation of the scheme itself is complicated but comparable to other, likewise multi-layered guestwork programmes operating in East and Southeast Asia (see Spaan and Hillmann 2013, 73–74; Xiang and Lindquist 2014, S128–132; Surak 2017). The transnational bureaucracy created by the Thailand–Myanmar MoU (Gruß 2017, 7) operates through agencies and brokers on both sides of the border (International Labour Organization 2015, 18). In Thailand, multiple documents are processed in the cycle of exchanges between the Thai employer, the Provincial Employment Office, Department of Employment (DOE, under the Ministry of Labour) in Bangkok and the Myanmar embassy (see International Labour Organization 2015, 12). In Myanmar, the counterpart of the DOE is the regional Labour Exchange Offices under the Ministry of Labour. The prospective Thai employer applies for a migrant labour quota, the Provincial Employment Office collects the requests, and Department of Employment approves them and communicates to the Myanmar embassy. When the selection process in Myanmar is complete, names of the applicants are sent to the DOE and the Thai workplace. The employer then confirms the acceptance of proposed workers so that the DOE can notify the Myanmar embassy and ask the Immigration Bureau to grant them a Thai visa. U Thant recalled waiting in Myawaddy for two or three months to obtain the documents, whereas Naw Eh Moo lost patience after two. Upon arrival in Thailand, workers undergo a medical test and apply for a Thai work permit. A broker may also be involved on the Thai side (International Labour Organization 2015, 19; Hall 2012, 6).

The Labour Exchange Offices in Myanmar are supposed to serve as pre-departure information and documentation centres. However, they outsource any active recruitment or training to licensed employment agencies and those operate through individual brokers affiliated with them. While waiting for his passport, U Thant—like migrants interviewed in Hall (2012)—ate and slept at his broker's house with other MoU applicants. When the migrants' number in the house hit 100, U Thant overnighted at a local Buddhist temple. At the Labour Exchange Office in Myawaddy, they just filled in the forms and were picked up on the day of departure. Such a layered structure inflates the fees as individual brokers, agencies and the officials all cut their share (see Hall 2012, 6), but are hard to hold accountable when something goes wrong, e.g., when it turns out that the employer does not exist or the worker does not accept the job upon arrival.

Apart from nominal temporary legality, the scheme does not necessarily offer protection to migrants. They are entitled to healthcare services in Thailand, social insurance and compensations for injuries sustained at work. However, Migrant Worker Rights Network, Myanmar Migrant Network Bangkok and MAP Foundation argue that the MoU workers face more restrictions and injustice than others. Their choice of employment is restricted, they may be promised jobs or conditions different from those that they actually find, and they cannot change employers who keep their documentation, effectively restricting their movement. In Myawaddy, U Thant and U Myo were given two types of jobs to choose from but not the name of their Thai employer—a construction company. The only contract they reported signing was with their broker and not the Thai employer. Upon arrival, their newly obtained passports were taken away in exchange for copies. The workers lived in employer-provided accommodation and were transported to the construction site every day but hardly went out otherwise despite being 'legal'. Already at the border were the migrants told that they must accept any responsibility for whatever happens to them if they leave without a passport. When stopped on the way back from work on a company truck, workers had to pay 500 THB each to appease the police officers. They were not earning more than the Thai legal minimum (300 THB a day) and could not change their employer without losing their work permit. Those who run away face arrest for violating their visa conditions (Hall 2012, 11). Their visa is for two years, renewable for another two. The renewal is not free of charge: U Thant and U Myo said they would need to pay a broker 16,000 THB each (471 USD).

The official Myanmar–Thailand low-paid labour migration channel has not displaced informal brokerage, becoming the less popular alternative instead. It is more expensive and does not guarantee more favourable work conditions—as it did not in South Korea of the 1990s (see Surak 2013, 96). It entails long waiting times, complete dependence on brokers and employers and restricted mobility. Although it is an official scheme involving state institutions, employment agencies and Thai employers, individual brokers are still migrants' interface. The multi-layered nature of the scheme adds to the costs and leaves migrants very constrained. The veil of legality obscures exploitative working conditions as the inter-governmental migrant export–import arrangement does not challenge the structures of the migrant labour market.

'Coming the Thief's Way'

It is clear that the 'legal' migration arrangements shape the relative attractiveness of the 'illegal' option. Due to their established networks, Karen migrants continue bypassing the MoU or going 'the thief's way', as they call it. It is brokers who ultimately supply the Thai labour market with Burmese workers—whether 'legal' or 'illegal'. Nearly all our interviewees from a village in central Kayin State who travelled to Thailand after 1995 did so with a broker (*pweza* in Burmese or *kely*—from the English 'carry' or 'carrier') at least for the first time. However, no case of human trafficking has been reported in the village for the past 10–15 years. How do their migration arrangements compare to those of the MoU process?

The fees charged by informal migration brokers are around 40% lower than the amounts MoU participants pay. This remains true despite their astounding rise since the mid-1990s when brokers had just recently emerged to satisfy growing demand. The Karen migrants' destinations were moving from the border areas into Thailand's interior at the same time as the Thai and Burmese authorities were tightening their control over the borderland. The figure of a mediator able to cut large-scale deals with the authorities to secure undocumented passage became unavoidable and, like elsewhere, fees kept rising as the risk undertaken by human smugglers grew (cf. Andreas 2001, 118). U Naing Min who worked as a broker from the mid-1990s to early 2000s initially charged 600 THB (worth 24 USD at the time) per person to get from the border to the workplace inland by car. Eventually, his fee rose to 2500 baht (59 USD after the Asian financial crisis). By 2000, Karen migrants were paying 6000–9000 baht (150–225 USD) to reach cities in Central Thailand. In the early 2010s, most recent arrivals we interviewed had paid 12,000–16,000 baht (375–500 USD) from the Thai border town of Mae Sot to Bangkok by car. In November 2016, according to updates by U Naing Min and Saw Mike Thar, a long-term migrant in Thailand, prices had declined and ranged between 10,000 and 12,000 THB (294–353 USD, see reason below). These are upfront fees for travel, accommodation and food on the way. Except for small amounts for the transport from Hpa-an to Myawaddy, no other fees are due to the broker or state officials. Smuggling brokers active among the Karen are usually not responsible for securing a job, accommodation at the destination and obtaining documents but they can assist in these matters too.

The travel arrangements, though risky, are much faster. They involve several actors but the relationships between them are informal, personal and based on trust. With no documents to obtain, villagers from Hpa-an Township in Myanmar can reach Bangkok within days. Three decades of Karen migration means that most new migrants have relatives or friends working in Thailand who can inform them of a job opportunity, offer temporary accommodation and recommend a broker who has safely transported them (cf. Wee and Sim 2004, 182–183; but see Molland 2012, 133–134). The broker arranges a car to Myawaddy. In the late 1990s and 2000s, it was also the broker's job to negotiate (and bribe if needed) the Burmese immigration officers manning multiple roadside checkpoints along the way to the border. The group crosses the interstate boundary marked by the River Moei (Thaung Yin) with the broker: by boat or wading on foot at an informal border crossing or sometimes through the official checkpoint by getting day passes that require only a Myanmar citizen ID card. On the Thai side, the Burmese broker transfers the group to the care of a cooperating Thai broker.

The most challenging task is to pass or avoid the Thai police checkpoints along the road leading from the border towards Bangkok. Several such checkpoints exist for inspecting passengers' documents between Mae Sot and the provincial centre of Tak. The solution depends on how well-connected the broker is. Among the Karen migrants, stories of travelling with many other people concealed in cargo trucks (where some have suffocated) or walking around the checkpoints through the mountains at night on foot seem to belong to the past. Most of our interviewees who came around or after the late 2000s did so in a 'police car' (a car belonging or driven by a collaborating Thai policeman), though some still had to be disguised in some way. Changing cars, staying at safe houses and regrouping are common. A 'police car' is considered the fastest and safest mode. In a 'police car', migrants can cover the distance between Mae Sot and Bangkok in one night. The popularity of this method suggests that most brokers have turned to collaborating with contacts within the Thai police manning the checkpoints. Most of the broker fee increases over time is due to kickbacks to the Thai immigration police. At the beginning, U Naing Min would pay the Thai police 500 THB out of the 600 THB he got per person. Later, the police would claim 2000 THB out of 2500 THB. If this breakdown is (still) representative, police collaborators get 4/5 or 5/6 of the broker fees.

Undocumented Karen border crossers see the risk as the matter of choosing a 'good' broker who cares for their safety rather than a 'bad' one who exploits their vulnerability (see also Labour Rights Promotion Network and Johns Hopkins School of Public Health Center for Refugee and Disaster Response 2011, 21; Sakaew and Tangpratchakoon 2009, 26). Although undocumented migrants are still vulnerable to police harassment, extortion and labour rights violations, MoU workers are exposed to similar injustice despite being 'legal'. Although most of Burmese migrant workers are smuggled into the country, much fewer could be considered victims of human trafficking (Labour Rights Promotion Network and Johns Hopkins School of Public Health Center for Refugee and Disaster Response 2011, 42–43). Human trafficking into Thailand does happen[8] but, among our Karen interviewees, cases when a person had been sold to a Thai employer and had to run away from abuse made up a tiny minority. All happened in women's first jobs as domestic workers in the late 1990s or early 2000s[9]. A village elder told us in 2012 that it was widespread a decade ago but we found no recent cases. Numbers of 'bad brokers' seem to have diminished at the same time as their relative position of power among the Karen. Growing migrants' financial capacity, connections and eligibility for post-arrival 'legalisation' (explored in the next section) are factors of their improved situation despite irregular migration status.

An elaborate system also exists to facilitate the departure of undocumented migrants. Although it is not cheaper than travelling 'legally', it is definitely faster than being arrested, detained and deported. As an officer of MAP Foundation officer pointed out in 2012, immigration detention centres have limited space and deportations are not conducted daily (see also Al Jazeera 2010). Therefore, arrested migrants can bribe themselves out: the earlier they pay, the more they save (see Soe Lin Aung 2019, 93). Judging from our interviews, brokered deportations have taken place since at least the mid-1990s. Undocumented Karen migrants would use them strategically to travel back to Myanmar. They would get in touch with their broker and take a passenger night bus to Mae Sot. At the first police checkpoint in the Tak border province, passengers without satisfactory documents are

---

[8] Human Rights Watch (2010, 52–56) and Labour Rights Promotion Network and Johns Hopkins School of Public Health Center for Refugee and Disaster Response (2011) provide some case studies.

[9] Pim Koetsawang (2001, 63–73, 116–123) also reports many individual stories of debt bondage from approximately the said period (1993–1998).

escorted off the bus. As the long-time migrant and my co-researcher Mu Tyhee explained, migrants are then detained in an enclosure till morning when their broker's representative arrives, collects money from the broker's clients as required and settles the accounts with the police. The group then boards an arranged pick-up truck to the River Moei and takes the boat across rather than exiting through the official border checkpoint on the bridge. Established broker–police relations facilitate mass-scale solutions at busy times like the Buddhist New Year holidays or emergencies. During the floods of 2011, thousands of migrants rushed back from Thailand to Myanmar. Busloads of workers were going to the border daily. According to Sa Than Win Aye, one such returnee, those with a broker paid 4000 THB (125 USD at the time) and an extra 200 THB (6.25 USD) as a bribe at the police checkpoint (so as not to be taken off the bus). Those with less cash could simply report themselves to a police station and would be deported for 2500 THB (78 USD).

Although undocumented migrants can face extortion when being deported, hiring a broker in advance helps avoid that. When deported outside the official checkpoint, migrants cross the border into the area on the Burmese side that is controlled by the Democratic Karen Buddhist Army[10] (Al Jazeera 2010). During the 2011 floods, migrants were reportedly being deported at night (when the border is officially closed) and forced to pay up to 4000 THB to the DKBA or Burmese border guards (*Bangkok Post* 2011), probably as they had not pre-arranged their trip. Reports (HRW 2010, 68–71; State Enterprise Workers Relations Confederation, Human Rights and Development Foundation, Thai Labour Solidarity Committee 2010) have documented a racketeering scheme involving the Thai immigration police, DKBA and the brokers. The Thai police basically sells the data of persons to be deported to brokers so that those can extort fees from the migrants, threatening with sanctions from DKBA if they do not pay. If migrants have no money, they are held to ransom or do forced labour. A representative of MAP Foundation confirmed that deportations through the DKBA checkpoint were taking place as of 2016, with the DKBA and the Thai authorities sharing the spoils. The rise of the police–broker–DKBA borderland nexus controlling the undocumented exit from Thailand has enabled the development of the scheme. However, none of the recent

---

[10]DKBA—a Karen militia that split from the Karen National Union (KNU) in 1994 after protracted insurgency against the Burmese central government (1948–2012). DKBA has been an unstable ally of the government ever since.

Karen migrants we interviewed mentioned falling prey, even if travelling undocumented, as they would use their familiar brokers.

It is evident that undocumented arrivals are as heavily brokered as those through the MoU programme. Since the 1990s, brokerage networks have entangled the border crossings, building alliances with Burmese and Thai immigration authorities as well as the DKBA militia. Circumventing the official employment agencies and hiring a trusted human smuggler cuts through the red tape and decreases the fees due. Along with internal migration, MoU is considered a good opportunity in the communities of central Myanmar where its brokerage networks are stronger than those of human smuggling agents. The latter are widespread in the borderlands with a developed cross-border migration culture. There MoU is considered only when other options appear exhausted: otherwise, the guestwork scheme looks like state extortion rather than a safer and more transparent option. When it comes to undocumented departures, an advance arrangement with a familiar agent also helps to avoid delays and extortion. In either case, migration services are a commodity where legality comes at a high premium and at the expense of personal freedom. Undocumented migrants who can rely on their own networks for finding jobs in Thailand enjoy more flexibility, including the possibility to 'legalise' after arrival.

'Legalisation' and Staying 'Legal'

Intermittent availability of 'legalisation' after an undocumented arrival contributes to the limited success of the MoU process. Over time, the two tracks of migration blur into one in terms of costs, precariousness and methods used. For migrants already in Thailand, there have been two types of 'legalisation', their conditions also shaping each other's popularity. Migrant labour registration regularises migrants' employment but not their immigration status, whereas the so-called 'nationality verification' regularises both employment and immigration status for a certain period. Especially during its last rounds of registration, it was possible to conclude registration without a broker but the 'nationality verification' is a complicated and heavily brokered process. As rules and requirements are not transparent and keep changing, brokers play an important role in mediating the procedures, managing uncertainties but also claiming their share, even fraudulently. Although considered an asset, regularised (but always temporary) status means facing regular bureaucratic hoops and uncertainty as regulations are in flux.

Often in combination with sweeping arrests, Thai authorities have been experimenting with migrant labour registration or amnesties for undocumented foreign workers since 1992 with mixed results. An ad hoc Cabinet resolution would announce a period of a month or more for undocumented Burmese, Lao and Cambodian workers to register themselves, obtaining a 'migrant worker' or the so-called 'pink card'. If migrants miss the deadline, if the next round is announced after their cards have expired or if it only renews earlier registrations (as some rounds have), many migrants stay undocumented. Alternatively, workers may consider that the costs of registration outweigh its benefits and decide to forego it (see Caouette and Pack 2002, 29–30; Arnold 2005, 288). During the last round of April 2016, registration cost 7500 THB (214 USD) and cards issued were valid for two years (National News Bureau of Thailand 2014). Registration does not regularise the applicants' visa status but issues temporary residence and work permits, postponing deportation[11] (see Sciortino and Punpuing 2009b, 20–21, 55; Saltsman 2012, 10; Pearson and Kusakabe 2012, 178). Workers have health and social insurance but are registered in the province of residence and cannot travel outside of it without a special permission. During the last round, registration was rather straightforward as publicity and one-stop service centres with interpreters diminished the need for brokers' assistance. However, in the past, brokers have apparently tricked some ignorant migrants offering to register them for a fee when the registration was actually not available (Sakaew and Tangpratchakoon 2009, 17). In other cases, brokers arrange what should be impossible, e.g. help 'pink card' holders to travel without the required paperwork (see below).

Since 2009, registered migrant workers originating from Myanmar can undergo 'nationality verification' and obtain temporary passports during the announced window periods. They are granted a temporary work permit ('pink card') as they start the process, renewable upon its successful completion. Those passports were initially valid for three and most recently for up to six years.[12] For previously disenfranchised workers from Myanmar, 'nationality verification' has allowed to regularise and visit their home communities without spending lots of money on broker assistance. However,

---

[11] Srawooth Paithoonpong and Yongyuth Chalamwong (2012, 9–14) even use the term 'registered illegal migrant workers' to describe those who undergo the procedure.

[12] In 2014, a new scheme of cooperation of Thai and Burmese authorities started offering permanent passports to Burmese people working in Thailand but, like the MoU, it relies on a complex process (Nyein 2014).

the passport is not valid outside Thailand and the process of obtaining it is costly and complex, its structure resembling the MoU cycle (see IOM 2014). Migrants' data are supplied to Burmese authorities so that passports can be issued. During the first rounds of 'nationality verification', migrants themselves had to travel to Myanmar border towns for paperwork and would then cross back into Thailand 'legally' with their newly issued papers. The system allowed brokerage to thrive. Twelve official Thai agencies were contracted to mediate the process, but, like with the MoU process, the actual casework was done by private brokers operating in the agencies' name (see Gruß 2017). In 2012–2013, most workers we interviewed had already obtained temporary passports. New arrivals, though smuggled to Greater Bangkok, would acquire documentation within a year. All our interviewees seemed to have paid a different sum for the procedure. In 2013, Nan Thiri said that a temporary passport should cost 4800–5000 THB (150–156 USD at the time) but agencies charged even 12,000 THB (375 USD). In 2010, a guidance note from the Thai Department of Employment announced that the fee for middlemen services should not exceed 500 THB (16 USD) but did not enforce it (Huguet 2014, 20).

When 'pink cards' were available, some migrants preferred them as a cheaper alternative to the costly temporary passports. However, in March 2017, it was announced that all pink card holders had to obtain passports and visas or become undocumented (Pratch Rujivanarom 2017). 'Nationality verification' has not been available on an ongoing basis either. Between the rounds of several months (in practice repeatedly extended), information would be lacking, leaving migrants in the dark about what to expect as their documents expire: mass arrests and deportation or another amnesty and a new round of registration. In late 2013, the first temporary passports issued in 2009 were nearing expiry but there was no news if there would be any opportunities to renew the documents. Some migrants—like Naw Eh Moo—went back and applied to join the MoU programme, thinking that other options were exhausted. Many stayed on or came back undocumented like she did. While authorities were silent, brokers were the only source of insider information (or rumours).

Even long-term, experienced migrants fluent in Thai and Burmese struggle to obtain reliable information from Thai immigration authorities or Myanmar embassy in Thailand. In October 2016, nobody could tell my co-researcher Nan Sandar Aye how to switch from a 'pink card' to a passport now that her first temporary passport had long expired. At the time, immigration authorities in Bangkok would not stamp a visa into a newly acquired temporary passport of a 'pink card' holder but those in the neighbouring Samut Prakan province were doing it. With no prior announcement, it became possible in Bangkok a few weeks later. Meanwhile, the Myanmar embassy's consular section was basically run by brokers, Nan Sandar Aye complained. Brokers rather than consular officers would handle migrants' queries, not allowing them to deal with authorities themselves. Nan Sandar Aye and her husband, both fluent and literate in Burmese, filled in their forms themselves but still had to pay 500 THB to a broker. Both uncertainty and overt pressure make migrants seek brokers' services to keep emotional distance (Gruß 2017) from the tiring and humiliating procedures.

The Process of Managing Legality

Legality is a process continuously in the making (De Genova 2002). It requires ongoing effort, repeated investments and sometimes not-so-legal solutions. Thai bureaucratic requirements of legal status management include ninety-day reports and re-entry permits. Both procedures are mediated by brokers, with some of their solutions blurring the legal/illegal boundary. All foreigners legally residing in Thailand must report to an immigration centre every 90 days.[13] Holders of temporary passports and 'pink cards' go to centres reserved for low-paid Burmese, Lao and Cambodian employees. Migrants queue for the whole day or pay 200–300 THB to a broker to get the stamp in 15 minutes. Regularised migrants also need a special permission to travel back to their countries of origin. Temporary passport holders must go to an immigration centre, queue and pay 1000 THB (31 USD) for a re-entry permit—a stamp in their passport to be checked at police roadside checkpoints on the way to the border and at the immigration booth at exit. As usual, fast track is available for a higher fee (1500 THB or 47 USD). Missing re-entry permits and even Thai exit stamps (after an undocumented exit) can also be bought at the border retrospectively directly at immigration or through a broker.

Requirements are more stringent for 'pink card' holders. To obtain a re-entry permit, they need to submit a police form filled in by their employers and a recommendation letter from the Myanmar embassy. Some migrants would just hire a broker to leave clandestinely for 3000 THB (86 USD) instead. To re-enter Thailand afterwards, brokers' fees are lower: according

---

[13] Some Thai employers undertake the responsibility to manage the paperwork.

to U Naing Ming, 'pink card' holders would pay 8000–9000 THB (229–257 USD) in October 2016. Thai immigration police who officially forbid the 'pink card' holders to travel freely, actually allowed them to do so with the broker's intervention, recognising them as semi-documented. As brokers mixed semi-documented and undocumented migrants to outsmart the police, the rates went down for the latter too (see above).

It is evident that the boundary between documented and undocumented migration tracks is not clear-cut. The availability of 'legalisation' after arrival demonstrates that (il)legality is a process that requires constant management, creating opportunities for brokerage. 'Legalisation' offers the conversion to legal status without the MoU conditions but it also creates the in-between category of being semi-documented—'pink card' holders that may or may not become fully documented in future. Some brokered solutions for legal status maintenance also bridge the narrow gap between the 'legal' and 'illegal'. Formal and informal border crossing channels coexist and intertwine as migrants use them strategically. Most moves are possible for a fee—to the broker or to the immigration official mediating the strict regulations.

Conclusion

In a recent volume on migration industries, Surak (2013, 94) suggests that they are more powerful in 'legal' than in 'illegal' migration, whereas Hernández-León (2013, 31–32) talks of 'bastard industry' of extortion, trafficking and kidnapping spawned by strict state policies against unauthorised flows. Migration industries producing documented migrants and 'bastard industries' developing in criminal spaces seem to be at the opposite ends of the spectrum of legality. Yet in the Myanmar–Thailand migration, they exist side by side and sometimes overlap. In the Karen borderland, 'trafficking' and 'extortion' are as likely to refer to the state-sanctioned guestwork scheme as they are to DKBA's deportation racket. Migration industry runs both the 'legal' and 'illegal' migration track and the state agents—officially or under cover—actively control and sanction both. Whether a state institution is the chief broker shepherding migrants through the narrow and heavily guarded gate or its agents look the other way when heavy undocumented flows seep through other sections of the porous border, the state is complicit. Whether Burmese migrants move over or under the bridge, state agents are prominent in the migration industry and implicated in thick brokerage networks.

The tight alliance developed as the Burmese and Thai state institutions gradually extended their grip over the restive borderland. Tightening border enforcement necessitated the rise of migration brokers, growing the stakes and costs. Since the 1990s, brokerage has become ingrained in the management of low-paid labour migration to Thailand from neighbouring countries. When 'legal' migration was not available, fixers brokered the missing transborder infrastructure, mediating between migrants and state agents on the one hand and between the Burmese and Thai state agents on the other. Only in 2009 did a transborder bureaucracy emerge, creating a 'legal' channel of labour import and a process of 'legalisation' of workers already in Thailand. However, the multi-tiered MoU bureaucracy cannot function without official agencies and individual brokers—the migrants' interface. Today brokers are involved in many aspects of migrant lives, mediating both the 'legal' and 'illegal' channels of migration, status conversion and its day-to-day management.

Regularising migrants is believed to protect them from exploitation but it does not necessarily do so (cf. Molland 2012, 118, 121). The Thai government has repeatedly stated its aim to root out illegality and channel all low-paid labour migration via the cumbersome MoU process. However, a comparison of the MoU programme and undocumented migration to Thailand simply as migrant-exporting schemes reveals why McKeown (2012, 43) calls guestwork the other side of human trafficking. Despite vilifying migration brokers, the state can be a broker and a 'bad' one. The state and market intermingle in managing and taxing migrants. On the migration market, price and other conditions attached to the 'legal' and 'illegal' channels and to the two types of 'legalisation' influence their relative attraction. However, information asymmetry exists as borderland communities are more aware of the alternative tracks and the price of legality on arrival.

Both migration tracks and their intersections are commercialised and brokered. Legality, too, is an expensive asset of sometimes marginal benefit that requires maintenance under uncertain and evolving conditions. It is co-produced by the state agents, brokers and migrants themselves. All actions come at a price. Participants of the MoU scheme pay high fees upfront, whereas undocumented migrants accrue expenses legalising and maintaining their status (or bribing the police when arrested). Undocumented migrants pay (the brokers and brokers pay) the immigration police manning checkpoints, whereas regularised workers pay the immigration officers. Either way, an official or unofficial authorisation is obtained and fees to brokers and/or the state agents acting as brokers are paid. Sometimes, only the resulting migrants' (il)legal status at arrival differentiates the tracks.

The encompassing, resilient and diversified industry facilitating and controlling migration operates across the spectre of (il)legality. When status is seen as a process, the boundary between being documented and undocumented becomes blurred. Status conversion is possible, and there are grey areas. Intermittent availability of 'legalisation' after arrival contributes to the limited success of the MoU and creates the semi-documented status. Given the time restrictions and unstable regulation, it is easy to lapse into illegality. There are nuances to (il)legality and the Karen prefer the flexible legality resulting from 'nationality verification' to the nominal and restraining legality bestowed by the official guestwork scheme. Finally, the management of legality may require 'illegal' methods.

Acknowledgements The author would like to thank her gatekeepers, co-researchers, research participants and sponsors as well as the participants of the 'The Migration Industry' workshop at NUS in June 2017 where she presented a draft of the paper.

References

Al Jazeera. (2010, July 17). *Migrants caught in vicious cycle*. http://www.aljazeera.com/video/asia-pacific/2010/07/201071723514942402.html?utm=from_old_mobile.

Alpes, M. J. (2013). *Law and the credibility of migration brokers: The case of emigration dynamics in Cameroon*. International Migration Institute Working Papers Series 80. Oxford: University of Oxford. http://www.ohchr.org/Documents/Issues/Migration/StudyMigrants/CivilSociety/JillAlpesMigrationbrokers.pdf.

Alpes, M. J. (2017). *Brokering high-risk migration and illegality in West Africa: Abroad at any cost*. Studies in Migration and Diaspora. Oxford and New York: Routledge.

Ananta, A., & Arifin, E. N. (2004). Should Southeast Asian borders be opened? In A. Ananta & E. N. Arifin (Eds.), *International migration in Southeast Asia* (pp. 1–27). Singapore: ISEAS Institute of Southeast Asian Studies.

Andreas, P. (2001). The transformation of migrant smuggling across the U.S.-Mexican Border. In D. Kyle & R. Koslowski (Eds.), *Global human smuggling: Comparative perspectives* (pp. 107–125). Baltimore and London: John Hopkins University Press.

Arnold, D. (2005). The situation of Burmese migrant workers in Mae Sot, Thailand. In D. Chang & E. Shepherd (Eds.), *Asian transnational corporation outlook 2004: Asian TNCs, workers, and the movement of capital, by Asia Monitor Resource Centre* (pp. 287–329). Asian TNC Monitoring Network Book Series. Hong Kong: Asia Monitor Resource Centre. http://amrc.org.hk/text/system/files/ATNC-2004.pdf#page=300.

Bangkok Post. (2011, November 13). Cast Adrift. Teak Door. http://teakdoor.com/thailand-and-asia-news/97694-the-politics-behind-thailands-floods-38.html.

Caouette, T. M., Artchavanitkul, K., & Pyne, H. H. (2000). *Sexuality, reproductive health and violence: Experiences of migrants from Burma in Thailand*. Nakhonprathom: Institute for Population and Social Research, Mahidol University at Salaya.

Caouette, T. M., & Pack, M. E. (2002). *Pushing past the definitions: Migration from Burma to Thailand*. Refugees International & Open Society Foundation. http://www.refworld.org/docid/47a6eb9d0.html.

Castles, S. (2004). The myth of the controllability of difference: Labour migration, transnational communities and state strategies in the Asia-Pacific region. In B. S. A. Yeoh & K. Willis (Eds.), *State/nation/transnation: Perspectives on transnationalism in the Asia-Pacific* (pp. 16–36). Transnationalism 12. London and New York: Routledge.

Castles, S., de Haas, H., & Miller, M. J. (2014). *The age of migration: International population movements in the modern world* (5th ed.). New York and London: Guilford Press.

Cranston, S., Schapendonk, J., & Spaan, E. (2017). New directions in exploring the migration industries: Introduction to special issue. *Journal of Ethnic and Migration Studies, 44*(4), 1–15.

Ditmore, M., & Wijers, M. (2003). The negotiations on the UN Protocol on trafficking in persons. *Nemesis, 4,* 79–88.

Genova, D., & Nicholas, P. (2002). Migrant "illegality" and deportability in everyday life. *Annual Review of Anthropology, 31,* 419–447.

Gruß, I. (2017). The emergence of the temporary migrant: Bureaucracies, legality and Myanmar migrants in Thailand. *SOJOURN: Journal of Social Issues in Southeast Asia, 32*(1), 1–35.

Hall, A. (2012). *Experiences of Myanmar migrant workers in Thailand with the MoU import process*. Mahidol Migration Centre at Mahidol University Institute for Population and Social Research. http://oppenheimer.mcgill.ca/IMG/pdf/Experiences_of_Myanmar_Migrant_Workers_in_Thailand_with_the_MoU_Import_Process.pdf.

Hernández-León, R. (2013). Conceptualizing the migration industry. In T. Gammeltoft-Hansen & N. N. Sørensen (Eds.), *The migration industry and the commercialization of international migration*. Global Institutions Series. London and New York: Routledge.

HRW. (2010). *From the tiger to the crocodile: Abuse of migrant workers in Thailand*. Human Rights Watch. http://www.hrw.org/sites/default/files/reports/thailand0210webwcover_0.pdf.

Huguet, J. W. (2014). Thailand migration profile. In J. W. Huguet (Ed.), *Thailand migration report 2014* (pp. 1–11). Bangkok: United Nations Thematic Working Group on Migration in Thailand. http://th.iom.int/images/report/TMR_2014.pdf.

International Labour Organization. (2015). *Review of the effectiveness of the MOUs in managing labour migration between Thailand and neighbouring countries.* Tripartite Action to Protect the Rights of Migrant Workers within and from the Greater Mekong Subregion (GMS TRIANGLE Project). Bangkok: ILO Regional Office for Asia and the Pacific. http://www.ilo.org/wcmsp5/groups/public/—asia/—ro-bangkok/documents/publication/wcms_356542.pdf.

IOM. (2014). Migrant information note. *Migrant information note 25.* Bangkok: International Organization for Migration, Thailand Office. http://thailand.iom.int/sites/default/files/document/publications/Migration%2BInformation%2B25%2BENG.pdf.

Kern, A., & Müller-Böker, U. (2015, October). The middle space of migration: A case study on brokerage and recruitment agencies in Nepal. *Geoforum, 65*, 158–169.

Khosravi, S. (2010). *'Illegal' traveller: An auto-ethnography of borders* (1st ed.). Global Ethics Series. Basingstoke: Palgrave Macmillan.

Koetsawang, P. (2001). *In search of sunlight: Burmese migrant workers in Thailand.* Bangkok, Thailand: Orchid Press.

Kyle, D., & Siracusa, C. A. (2005). Seeing the state like an migrant: Why so many non-criminals break immigration laws. In W. van Schendel & I. Abraham (Eds.), *Illicit flows and criminal things: States, borders, and the other side of globalization* (pp. 153–176). Tracking Globalization Series. Bloomington, Indianapolis: Indiana University Press.

Labour Rights Promotion Network, and Johns Hopkins School of Public Health Center for Refugee and Disaster Response. (2011). *Estimating labor trafficking: A study of Burmese migrant workers in Samut Sakhon, Thailand.* Bangkok: United Nations Inter-Agency Project on Human Trafficking. http://www.no-trafficking.org/reports_docs/estimates/uniap_estimating_labor_trafficking_report.pdf.

Lan, P. C. (2007). Legal servitude and free illegality: Migrant "guest" workers in Taiwan. In R. S. Parreñas & L. C. D. Siu (Eds.), *Asian diasporas: New formations, new conceptions* (pp. 253–277). Stanford: Stanford University Press.

Lin, W., Lindquist, J., Xiang, B., & Yeoh, Brenda S. A. (2017). Migration infrastructures and the production of migrant mobilities. *Mobilities, 12*(2), 167–174.

Lindquist, J., Xiang, B., & Yeoh, Brenda S. A. (2012). Introduction: Opening the black box of migration—Brokers, the organization of transnational mobility and the changing political economy in Asia. *Pacific Affairs, 85*(1), 7–19.

Ma, A. (2017, January 18). *Labor migration from Myanmar: Remittances, reforms, and challenges.* Migration Policy Institute. http://www.migrationpolicy.org/article/labor-migration-myanmar-remittances-reforms-and-challenges.

McKeown, A. M. (2008). *Melancholy order: Asian migration and the globalization of borders.* Columbia Studies in International and Global History. New York: Columbia University Press.

McKeown, A. (2012). How the box became black: Brokers and the creation of the free migrant. *Pacific Affairs, 85*(1), 21–45.

Molland, S. (2012). Safe migration, dilettante brokers and the appropriation of legality: Lao-Thai "trafficking" in the context of regulating labour migration. *Pacific Affairs, 85*(1), 117–136.

Natali, C., McDougall, E., & Stubbington, S. (2014). 'International migration policy in Thailand'. In J. W. Huguet (Ed.), *Thailand migration report 2014* (pp. 13–24). Bangkok: United Nations Thematic Working Group on Migration in Thailand. http://th.iom.int/images/report/TMR_2014.pdf.

National News Bureau of Thailand. (2014, April 2). *One-stop service centers reopen for migrant worker registration.* Mekong Migration Network. http://www.mekongmigration.org/?p=4922.

National Wages and Productivity Commission. (2019, April 30). *Comparative wages in selected countries.* Department of Labor and Employment National Wages and Productivity Commission. http://www.nwpc.dole.gov.ph/stats/comparative-wages-in-selected-countries/.

Nyein, N. (2014, March 21). *Myanmar begins passport scheme for migrant workers in Thailand.* The Irrawaddy. http://www.irrawaddy.org/burma/burma-begins-passport-scheme-migrant-workers-thailand.html.

Paithoonpong, S., & Chalamwong, Y. (2012). *Managing international labor migration in ASEAN: A case of Thailand.* Bangkok: Thailand Development Research Institute.

Pearson, R., & Kusakabe, K. (2012). *Thailand's hidden workforce: Burmese migrant women factory workers.* Asian Arguments. London and New York: Zed Books, Palgrave Macmillan.

Pratch Rujivanarom. (2017, May 1). New work permit rules make for an uncertain May Day for migrant workers. *The Nation.* http://www.nationmultimedia.com/news/national/30313852.

Sakaew, S., & Tangpratchakoon, P. (2009). *Brokers and labor migration from Myanmar: A case study from Samut Sakorn.* Labour Rights Promotion Network, Social Research Institute and Asian Research Center for Migration. Chulalongkorn University. http://www.arcmthailand.com/documents/publications/lpn-en.pdf.

Salt, J., & Stein, J. (1997). Migration as a business: The case of trafficking. *International Migration, 35*(4), 467–494.
Saltsman, A. (2012). *Surviving or thriving on the Thai-Burma border: Vulnerability and resilience in Mae Sot Thailand.* Bangkok: International Rescue Committee.
Sciortino, R., & Punpuing, S. (2009a). *International migration in Thailand 2009.* Bangkok: International Organization for Migration, Thailand Office. http://reliefweb.int/report/myanmar/international-migration-thailand-2009.
Sciortino, R., & Punpuing, S. (2009b). *International migration in Thailand 2009.* Bangkok: International Organization for Migration. http://www.ipsr.mahidol.ac.th/ipsr/Contents/Articles/2009/264-Internation-Migration-Thailand.pdf.
Soe Lin Aung. (2019). Notes on the Practice of Everyday Politics: Rereading the Labour of Self-Protection Among Migrant Communities on the Thai-Burma Border. *Journal of Social Sciences, Faculty of Social Sciences, Chiang Mai University, 24*(1–2), 63–114. https://www.tci-thaijo.org/index.php/jss/article/view/178102/126693.
Spaan, E., & Hillmann, F. (2013). Migration trajectories and the migration industry: Theoretical reflections and empirical examples from Asia. In T. Gammeltoft-Hansen & N. Nyberg Sørensen (Eds.), *The migration industry and the commercialization of international migration* (pp. 64–86). Global Institutions Series. London and New York: Routledge. https://www.routledge.com/The-Migration-Industry-and-the-Commercialization-of-International-Migration/Gammeltoft-Hansen-Nyberg-Sorensen/p/book/9780415623797.
State Enterprise Workers Relations Confederation, Human Rights and Development Foundation, Thai Labour Solidarity Committee. (2010). *Open letter requesting investigation of claims migrants deported from Thailand facing human rights abuses by DKBA.* Human Rights Watch. http://www.hrw.org/news/2010/07/19/open-letter-requesting-investigation-claims-migrants-deported-thailand-facing-human.
Surak, K. (2013). The migration industry and development states in East Asia. In T. Gammeltoft-Hansen & N. N. Sørensen (Eds.), *The migration industry and the commercialization of international migration* (pp. 87–107). Global Institutions Series. London and New York: Routledge. https://www.routledge.com/The-Migration-Industry-and-the-Commercialization-of-International-Migration/Gammeltoft-Hansen-Nyberg-Sorensen/p/book/9780415623797.
Surak, K. (2017, January). Migration industries and the state: Guestwork programs in East Asia. *International Migration Review* (Fall), 1–37.
Trading Economics. (2018a). Myanma Kyat. https://tradingeconomics.com/myanmar/currency.
Trading Economics. (2018b). Thai Baht. https://tradingeconomics.com/thailand/currency.

United Nations. (2000). *Protocol against the smuggling of migrants by land, sea and air, supplementing the United Nations convention against transnational organized crime.* https://www.unodc.org/documents/treaties/UNTOC/Publications/TOC%20Convention/TOCebook-e.pdf.

van Schendel, W. (2005). *The Bengal Borderland: Beyond state and nation in South Asia.* London: Anthem Press.

van Schendel, W., & Abraham, I. (2005). Introduction: The making of illicitness. In W. van Schendel & I. Abraham (Eds.), *Illicit flows and criminal things: States, borders, and the other side of globalization* (pp. 1–37). Tracking Globalization Series. Bloomington and Indianapolis: Indiana University Press.

Wee, V., & Sim, A. (2004). Transnational networks in female labour migration. In A. Ananta & E. N. Arifin (Eds.), *International migration in Southeast Asia* (pp. 166–198). Singapore: Institute of Southeast Asian Studies.

Xiang, B. (2012). Predatory Princes and Princely Peddlers: The state and international labour migration intermediaries in China. *Pacific Affairs, 85*(1), 47–68.

Xiang, B., & Lindquist, J. (2014, September). Migration infrastructure. *International Migration Review, 48,* S122–S148.

CHAPTER 4

Understanding the Cost of Migration: Facilitating Migration from India to Singapore and the Middle East

Michiel Baas

Introduction

When Lindquist et al. (2010) suggested to think of the middle space that connects sending and receiving nations as a black box which migration research had a task to pry open in order to understand its functioning, they argued that a focus on brokers is a productive way of doing so. While an increasing number of studies have paid heed to this call, a question which has received only scant attention so far is how those active in the migration industry fix the prices for the services they render. Research on low-skilled migrants in Asia frequently emphasizes the high cost of migration (e.g. Lindquist 2010; Goh et al. 2016; Rahman 2017). As a result, not seldom are migration trajectories financed by taking out considerable loans with possibly exploitative repayment schemes (see Goh et al. 2016). However, as my own research among variously skilled Indian migrants in Singapore also confirmed, the amounts paid to migrate abroad tend to vary considerably.

M. Baas (✉)
National University of Singapore, Singapore, Singapore
e-mail: arimba@nus.edu.sg

Drawing on extensive case material collected in the greater Chennai region of Tamil Nadu (India), this chapter investigates what determines the rates agents charge to low-skilled migrants[1] who desire to go to Singapore and the Middle East for work. It does so specifically by investigating this from the perspective of these agents themselves. The black box it seeks to engage with is not just represented by the vastly different amounts that low-skilled migrants from Tamil Nadu appear to pay to their respective agents, but by way of contrast also the rates quoted by Chennai-based agents themselves.

The scope of this chapter is threefold. First of all, the focus is on how migration agents discuss, formulate, and eventually fix the rates for their clients. The goal is not so much to arrive at a factual or precise overview of what determines the cost of migration—something which the inherent structuring of the industry makes nearly impossible—but to understand how the different actors involved in facilitating migration from Tamil Nadu to Singapore engage with this. Since most brokers active in the greater Chennai region cater to multiple migration destinations, the subsequent question this chapter engages with is how these various destinations compare to each other in terms of their cost structure. The query which, in simple terms, summarizes the investigation is how it is possible that it is relatively cheaper to migrate to destinations in the Middle East than it is to Singapore. As we will see, the cost structure of various migration destinations is not only determined by the various rates imposed by rules and regulation—an important reason why migration is relatively more expensive for those with low-skilled backgrounds than those of higher-skilled ones—but also by what these destinations are imagined to stand for in terms of livability, cultural closeness, and even brand-value. Finally, what this chapter contributes to is a better understanding of the consequences of the commercialization of migration trajectories as well as the implementation of protective (legislative) measurements by sending and receiving nations. While the intention of this article is not to argue that migration agents do not frequently engage in exploitative and/or illicit practices that allow them to profit from low-skilled migrant workers' precariousness, the overall argument is that there are multiple economic and social factors that contribute to the "price" of migration. In the conclusion, this chapter argues that in order to develop a better understanding of the underlying

---

[1] Although low skilled is common speak when referring to migrant workers in Singapore, the city-state itself employs semi-skilled as its preferred categorization. This is in contrast to mid-level and highly skilled migrants for which it has designated separate categories.

processes that shape the flow, form, and structure migration takes, the factor of money itself is crucial.

Methodology and Data

Conducting research among those active in the migration industry poses considerable constraints from the onset. For one, since the industry tends to be intensely competitive in terms of opportunities for brokerage, those in the business of facilitating migration are generally reluctant to provide insight into the functioning of their operations. Securing lucrative recruitment contracts to source migrant workers for clients in Singapore and other destinations and potentially significant earnings made from the migration desires of young lower-middle and labor-class men in Tamil Nadu are key to understanding this. Besides that, since agents often operate in the interstices between legal and illegal domains, negotiating contacts and contracts across nation states, and meeting as well as avoiding stringent rules and regulations at home as well as abroad, operations tend to rely on a high degree of confidentiality. These were undeniably issues I also faced while conducting research among agents and brokers in the greater Chennai region over the period of three months in 2016.

In total, I gathered data on fourteen migration agents while more informal conversations, which often took the form of semi-structured interviews, were conducted with a larger number. Within India's migration industry, the terms agents and brokers are used rather interchangeably with the exception that so-called *license holders* generally referred to themselves as agents and those who provided them with potential migrant workers as brokers, subagents, or subcontractors. As will be analyzed in greater detail below, license holders tend to be large-scale operations that hold an official and costly license to source migrants for Singaporean clients, something for which they make use of a battalion of sub(agents) who operate independently of them. I would generally meet these men[2] in the offices of the migration agents I had established formal relations with and who, on the

---

[2] Although no conclusive statistical data is available for this, it appears that Tamil migrant workers in Singapore are predominantly male. Since most end up working on construction sites or in the Singapore as harbor, this may not be a surprise. In contrast, the neighboring state of Kerala is a significant source of female migrants who find employment as migrant domestic workers in the Gulf. Because of the focus of my research, I predominantly met male agents, although the administrative staff would frequently consist of female employees as well.

guarantee of strict anonymity, had agreed to provide me with an insight into their business dealings. The reason I do not quantify the numbers of the second group of *subagents* is because such interactions often took place in the form of informal conversations in which informants would casually participate. These informal conversations often turned out to provide insightful information about the functioning of the migration industry though. The use of a research assistant who is fluent in Tamil was instrumental in making initial contact as well as offering assistance with translations when informants' English was too limited. Since this RA was himself an accomplished journalist, his investigative skills proved invaluable.[3]

While all informants were initially reluctant to cooperate to varying degrees, the opportunity to "set the record straight" was often articulated as part of their reason to participate in the research. For one, it quickly became clear that the relationship between license holders and (sub)agents was characterized by a precarious balance between trust and distrust. While the former would rely on the latter for low-skilled migrants that could be channeled to Singapore to meet a specific demand, the realization that license holders had little control over how subcontractors sourced their migrants also made them suspect in terms of the shadier dealings of the business. As license holders were keen to explain their "innocence" and emphasized their "righteousness" in doing business, they were also eager to vilify their subagents over which they appeared to have little control. It is this tension that informed the data gathering from the onset and which provided important insight into the complexities of low-skilled migrant worker recruitment and overseas placement. It is this complex relationship which I will seek to unpack further in the coming sections.

All interviews and conversations were conducted promising full anonymity. In this chapter, I will only refer to the agencies as I interacted with as Agency A, B, C, et cetera. All are based in the greater Chennai region which encompasses nearby villages and industrial areas. Although a few cater exclusively to the Singaporean market, the majority of agents source for markets as diverse as those from Southeast Asia to the Gulf and other countries in the Middle East. It is in particular this comparative perspective to the latter which provides insight into the costing of migration services. Table 4.1 provides a full overview of the agencies involved in the research.

---

[3] I would like to thank K. Ramesh Babu for this assistance here.

Table 4.1 Overview of agencies involved in the research

Agency[a]	Destinations	Visa types	Categories	Migrants per year (average)
A (License)	Multiple	Multiple	Multiple	?
B (Agent)	Multiple	Work Pass	Construction, harbor	?
C (License)	Multiple	Multiple	Drivers	300–400
D (License)	Singapore	Multiple	Construction	1000+
E (License)	Multiple	Multiple	Nurses, drivers	60–100
F (License)	Multiple	Multiple	Skilled. Prof. Construction	2–3 (Singapore)
G (License)	Multiple	Work Pass	Construction	?
H (License)	Singapore	S Pass	Nursing	100
I (License)	Singapore	Work Pass	Harbor	700–800
J (Training)	Gulf	Work Pass	Construction	?
K (Training)	Multiple	Work Pass	Harbor	300–500
L (License)	Multiple	Multiple	Skilled Prof.	?
M (Broker)	Gulf, Singapore	Work Pass	Construction	?
N (License)	Multiple	Student visa	Universities	?

[a]The column detailing "Agency" provides additional information between brackets: License means "license holder"; Agent means that this person does not hold a license; Training means that the "license holder" also operates a training institute. If "Destinations" says multiple, it means that this agent facilitates migration to multiple destinations, in general, these are The Middle East, Malaysia, and Singapore. If "Visa Types" says this refers to the multiple types of visas, it arranges for Singapore: ranging from Work Pass (for low- or semi-skilled workers) to S Pass (mid-level skilled) and E Pass (highly skilled). In general, though the bulk of visas will be of the Work Pass variety. "Categories" refers to the professional categories migrants are recruited in. "Average/year" gives information on the number of migrants the agent generally sends abroad. Agents were reluctant to give information on this for two reasons: confidentiality and difficulty to give a proper estimate due to changing market conditions

MIGRATION AGENTS IN TAMIL NADU

Agency B (Broker)

This agency is located in a remote corner of the city, in a small neighborhood which is part of the Pallavaram area of Chennai. Once a thriving hotspot of industries offering jobs to significant numbers of employees, today most of these jobs have relocated to the nearby IT corridor, a special zone where many Indian IT companies are now located. The owner of Agency B (Murali) originally hails from Pudukkottai and used to be employed as an administrative clerk, making up to Rs. 17,000 per month. When he got married, he felt this income would not be enough to sustain himself, his child, and his aging parents on. As a result, he starting looking for a "more lucrative career" as he put it himself. With his wife assisting him, he is now able to generate an income of around Rs. 50,000 per month. Although he functions as a migrant agent he is not registered with the Ministry and thus not a license holder. A license would set him back cost 10 lakhs,[4] something he assumed would soon be increased to 30 lakhs. Showing an impressive database in an excel sheet which he meticulously maintains, it boasts 1192 subagents on which he depends for new recruits. He sources for ten license holders, eight of which he is in direct contact with and two of which he caters to indirectly via another non-licensed agent.

Murali's revenue model thus depends on sourcing migrant workers in bulk for the various license holders he is in contact with. He provided me with the following example: "For a particular recruitment in bulk I may be having something which is numerically 50, to say, I may be having 25-30 on hand... But for the remaining numbers I have to gather them from my subagents." The migrants that he has "on hand" are those who have contacted him with their resumes and made inquiries after potentially working abroad. In a similar vein, subagents located in Tamil Nadu's (smaller) regional/provincial areas will contact him as well, offering their brokerage services. According to Murali, a Work Pass should cost a potential migrant between Rs. 1,30,000–1,80,000 which equals around S$2500-3750. He suggested his cut was a standard Rs. 10,000 but when asked what was included in the rest of the money remained somewhat unclear. The license holder, he was sure of, would take another Rs. 10,000. And other costs might include airfare, training, medical checks, and fees for the subagent. He agreed however that "adding it all up" was not easy.

Agency D (Training)

Agency D initially commenced their operations in the state of Andhra Pradesh (AP) after which they relocated to Tamil Nadu. Due to the competition for skilled migrants from Tamil Nadu, their main base for recruitment remains in Andhra Pradesh though. As they explained: "We expanded slowly and now operate with subagents across AP and Tamil Nadu." While talking to the office manager in charge (Kavya), several of these subagents walked in and joined the conversation. Kavya stressed that the recruitment

---

[4] A lakh is equal to Rs. 100,000.

is mainly done by word of mouth. Persons the agency has worked with before or their clients have "good experience with" are a usual source of potential migrant labor. "We also accept references from our ex-candidates only and will not accept fresh candidates." If the agency faces a shortage, they may advertise in local newspapers but only as a last resort.

Since 2007, the agency has solely been in the business of recruiting migrants for Singapore. Recruitment orders tend to come in bulk, and it is always a challenge to find the right match in terms of skills and experience. Kavya gave as an example a recent recruitment order of 94 persons; of the workers the agency had suggested to their Singaporean counterpart, 34 had been rejected for various reasons. In order to reduce the chance of having candidates rejected the agency prefers working with so-called U-turners who have been to Singapore before. Singapore-based clients tend to prefer these since they have already been exposed to Singaporean work standards and have completed their previous contract of 24 months. In order to make sure there is a direct match between the requirements of the Singaporean client and skills set of the migrant workers, the agency runs two training institutes in the outskirts of Chennai. At a time, 250 students can be accommodated here; a canteen and hostel are located on the grounds as well. Depending on the length of the course required, the agency charges Rs. 2000–5000. Furthermore, Kavya explained: "Post training skill evaluation tests will be conducted and client's HR will conduct interviews at the training venue itself." Since the institute often recruits workers who are not well-versed in the English language, English language training is part of the curriculum as well. "Training will be done on comprehensive writing pattern where passage will be provided and later questions will be asked from it."

The Work Permit holders this agency manages to send to Singapore make in-between S$400 and 1200. The Indian agency considers one month's salary there fee, while the Singaporean counterpart collects two months' salary. She went on to list certain stipulations that come with migrant worker contracts such as S$120 leave allowance if the worker does not take a day off per calendar month (besides the four days he is entitled to). In particular, it is working overtime that might make it worth going to Singapore. A workweek of 44 hours is the norm, but if there is an opportunity to work more "1.5 of basic salary will be paid." Furthermore, on public holidays salary is double.

Agency K (Training)

This agency is located in an industrial estate where, besides the office it operates, a large training center which prepares potential migrants for their employment abroad has also been established. They have been running the training institute for the last 15 years but have only recently gone into ITE training, providing certification courses specifically targeted at the Singaporean market. The training program they offer is conducted for up to 45 days, followed by an examination. For one month of training, the institute charges Rs. 15,000 per candidate. If the full 45 days is required, this might go up to Rs. 20,000. After finishing the course, the participants will return home and are subsequently asked to come for an interview when the actual recruitment process starts. They usually do so five days in advance to provide them with a refreshment course. A number of representatives of the Singaporean counterpart will be present for the recruitment process, interviewing the migrant candidates, and testing their knowledge of specific technique required for working in the Singaporean harbor (e.g., specific ways of welding, pipe laying, or safety regulations). The agent's main clients are shipyard based companies or oil and gas firms.

On average, a migrant worker is expected to spend two lakhs toward his employment overseas; of this amount, the agent (and license holder) in question takes one month's salary (minimum S$450). Furthermore, the agent was keen to stress that even though most of their workers have a starting salary of around S$450 per month, unless they are able to "make overtime" this salary would not be sufficient to consider actually going to Singapore. "They might as well stay here and get a job somewhere in Chennai if they will make that much." To this, the agent added that to make it worthwhile a migrant worker should make at least S$800, including overtime.

OPENING THE BLACK BOX

Based on the case studies above, it appears that migrating to Singapore for work should cost between 1.3 and 2 lakhs or S$2700 and 4200. However, it is important to note that this is the amount so-called license holders, or migration agents who are in direct contact and thus directly source to these license holders, quote. As we will see from the analysis below, the amount a migrant worker alleges to have paid to a migration agent usually also includes fees to subagents. Let me first provide a sketch of the various amounts that are generally included in the amount a license holding agency will quote. A helpful tool to double-check these amounts is an Employer's Copy of the In-Principle Approval for Work Permit (IPA) one agent gave me as an example. This in-principle approval is issued to the migrant worker stating that the migrant worker needs to enter Singapore before a specific set date. Besides stating the designated Occupation (Fork Lift Truck Operator) and full details of the migrant worker, it also lists his monthly salary, in this case S$484. Of this, there is a monthly food deduction of S$84 making the worker's "monthly salary after taking into account monthly allowances and deductions" S$400. It furthermore states that housing is provided and that a monthly levy rate of S$300 needs to be paid (by the employer). Finally, it informs the employer that the "Agency fee to be paid by the worker to Singapore Employment Agency (exclude fees for overseas expense) is S$800," basically the equivalent of two months' of salary excluding the contribution towards food. Based on this, the following "in principle" list can be compiled of various costs:

License holder	10,000	This is the usual "cut" the license holder takes if sourcing in bulk through dedicated agents
Chennai agent	25,000	The equivalent of one months' salary
Singapore agent	50,000	The equivalent of two months' salary
Papers	15,000	Various cost made to get official documents (e.g., birth certificates, diplomas) stamped, etc.
Medical	5000	Mandatory health screening before departure
Flight ticket	15,000	Chennai–Singapore one-way
Emigration	10,000	Various emigration related cost (agents were not willing to specify)
Training	20,000	Calculation for 45-days
Overhead	10,000	Rent, various office-related costs
Total	160,000	

If we look at the earlier mentioned variety of Rs. 1.3–2 lakhs or S$2700–4200, we see that the amount of 1.6 lakhs is squarely in the middle of this. However, it needs to be kept in mind that what it concerns here is an "ideal" depiction in which every separate item is accounted for. Yet migrant workers are known to frequently quote higher amounts. Besides that, not all receive full or partial training and some also indicated that they had to pay separately for items such as medical checks and air tickets. Moreover, for items such as Papers or Emigration, it is hard to assess what kind of costs is precisely included in this. If we work with a migrant agent's fee of S$5000, we see that around S$1600 or the equivalent of four months' of basic salary is not accounted for. *Where could this money have gone?* In the next section, I will discuss the way various license holders, brokers, and agents discuss this issue.

Adding up Agents

Initially, when I brought up the issue of inflated migrant agent fees, almost all of my informants reacted with a certain amount of concern. They emphasized that this was not the way they did business and that this was giving the industry as a whole a bad name. But they would also be quick to add that this is why they were keen to set the record straight. However, rarely did this actually happen. It was not so much that they were as puzzled as I was about the disconnect of amounts quoted and items paid for (either by the agent or by the migrant himself) but that it seemed those active in the business of migrant worker recruitment and placement had accepted a certain impenetrability of the industry. The way Agency B discussed this provides inside into what this means in practice. As a non-license holding agent, he relies on subagents to provide him with the necessary manpower. However, to this he added: "In this business, major problem is the attitude of subagents who play considerable role." According to him, this problem could be summarized as follows:

> Those agents just for money sake do lot of misdeeds. They cheat candidates and us badly. They promise candidates that the job is with all concessions and facilities. They are not showing original offer letter to the candidate and enter into forgery by signing candidate's signature through copying from the passport which they collect from the candidate for VISA arrangements. Hence candidate is not aware of exact offer and lands up in trouble while with the master. Subagents collects extra money from the candidate than what charged by the recruiter.

In general, the majority of migrants recruited do not hail from the Chennai region itself but from more regional and rural areas in the state. While spending time in the office of Agency D, one of their "base agents" walked in. "He brings in the manpower from regional areas," Kavya explained. Operating mainly in a southern part of Tamil Nadu, the agency pays him for every worker successfully recruited. In total, the agency works with thirty of such subagents. The way subagents work in their respective regional bases is by "referral" and entirely by word of mouth. This means that they will only "work with" migrants who are referred to them by (former) migrants who have been to Singapore before. Instrumental here is the issue of trust: for a Chennai-based license holder and/or agent, it is almost impossible to verify the skills and experience of a particular candidate beforehand, something for which they thus rely on for these subagents. A complicating factor, however, is that those based in Chennai often do not know who else is involved in the recruitment process. As it was suggested to me on more than one occasion, subagents might very well work with their own sub-subagents. Since there are no formal requirements "anyone can be an agent!" as one informant argued. Agency D made it quite explicit what they thought would be a solution here:

> Candidates must be aware of cheating and verify the VISA check up in respective embassies for genuineness of the company which recruits. I also suggest that the thumb impression from the candidate while signing in the offer letter. There should be proper mechanism for registration of subagents and direct job portals for overseas recruitments. Hence candidates can check up status of the job and other details of employer and migration agency.

While it is unlikely that such measures will be implemented anytime soon, it again underlines the tension that exists between large-scale agents/license holders and subagents.

The Problem of Overcharging

There are currently multiple pitfalls in the system which make overcharging possible without the direct "knowledge" of those holding the actual license to send migrants to Singapore. In order to better appreciate the complex nature of recruitment channels for migrant workers from Tamil Nadu, it helps to sketch this with a brief example from my fieldwork notes. In order to visit a recently returned S Pass migrant whom I knew from Singapore in his native town of Pudukkottai, I took the train from Villupuram near Pondicherry where I had been staying for a few days to reconnect with other contacts. Once in Pudukkottai, one quickly realizes one is in a much more provincial and rural part of Tamil Nadu. Still a sizable town of roughly 143,000 inhabitants, the surrounding area of much smaller towns is an important source for migrant workers. If a young man from one of these regional areas wishes to migrate abroad for work, he is likely to contact an agent in his native place. As I was assured through informal conversations with various migration agents, almost all of these smaller towns will have a regionally based person (sub-subagent) with whom people are familiar with and who is able to arrange/facilitate migration. However, for this to work, this contact person will rely on a contact in the nearest "bigger" town (Pudukkottai) who in turn might have a contact in the city of nearby Tiruchirappalli (better known as Trichy), which has over nine hundred thousand inhabitants. Although this agent might be a license holder and the route might thus stop there (since Trichy boasts an international airport with direct flights to Singapore among other destination), it is even more likely that the license holder is actually based in Chennai for administrative reasons. Adding up the number of agents involved comes down to four or perhaps even five (regionally based, Pudukkottai, Trichy, broker and/or license holder in Chennai); something which might contribute heavily to the ballooning of the final amount paid. Since the migrant worker often appears ill-informed of who the license holder is, or of what various elements the amount he is asked to pay is composed of, one can see how easy it is to overpay. If besides the agent and/or license holder take a cut of one month's salary (agent) and license holder (Rs. 10,000), four more salaries of one month can be accounted for, each ending up in the pockets of one of the other agents involved.

It needs to be stressed though that what I have attempted here is by and large speculation. None of the agents and license holders I interviewed involved were able or willing to confirm what I have sketched above. While license holders were relatively transparent in their dealings, claiming that their cut was usually Rs. 10,000, the further down the investigation reached the muddier the reasoning would get. This was not just because one did not appreciate my questioning in this regard but also because each person involved tended to keep their cards closely to their chests. One thing almost all agreed on, however, was that Singapore was decidedly more expensive as a migrant worker destination than the Middle East or the Gulf. In the next section, I will discuss how comparing migration destinations helps get a better sense of the various cost structures and also potentially clears up a particularly intangible aspect of migration costing.

Comparison Migration Destinations

Although the focus in my research was on agents who facilitate migration from Tamil Nadu to Singapore, most informants were keen to discuss how various migration destinations compared to each other. There were two reasons for this: One, most agents agreed that Singapore was a relatively problem-free migrant worker destination in terms of the treatment of migrants (compared to the Middle East). Two, it was generally also agreed that the Singaporean market for migrant workers was on a decline in terms of numbers. As a result, some agents except D, H, and I were now brokering for multiple destination and/or had gradually shifted their focus from Singapore to the Middle East (in particular, the Gulf).

Agency A was resolute in its opinion how the different destinations compared: "Cost wise Middle East is the right direction to get employed. Singapore is costlier and saving component is weak compared to the MEA." While income tax applied to migrant worker's salaries in Singapore, this agent suggested that since there was no "tax liability" in the Middle East, migrants would be able to save up to 50% of their salaries. Agency B was willing to make this more concrete by listing various amounts charged. Charging Rs. 40,000 for a candidate to go to the Gulf, it contrasted this with the 1.2–1.3 lakhs if the choice was Singapore. The amount for the Gulf includes the following: work accommodation card services (Rs. 3000); medical check (Rs. 4200), stamping duties (Rs. 7800); ticket (up to Sri Lanka,[5] Rs. 13,600); subagent fee (Rs. 5000), and profit margin for the agent himself (Rs. 6400). One reason the fee for the Gulf is so much lower, the agent argued, has to do with the mandatory involvement of the Singaporean counterpart for migration to Singapore, which equals two months' salary. But the next Agent (C) I spoke to also argued that cultural closeness also factored in the reason why Singapore remained popular with Tamil migrants and thus also why migrants were willing to pay more to go there:

> First one relatives and friends would be there. Second payment is prompt. Singapore itself has Tamil population so cultural practices are identical. Unlike Gulf climate is also pleasant. Under push factors here salary is restricted and limited comparatively they earn more in Singapore and if they do more hours of work they can earn more.

---

[5]The idea is that it is cheaper to fly to Sri Lanka and then onward to the Middle East. The subsequent ticket is not included in this calculation and is the responsibility of the migrant himself.

Other agents agreed with this. Agency J for instance stated that "Tamil Nadu candidates prefer Singapore against Gulf due to cultural and climatic reasons." While Agency C admitted that the standard of living was costlier in Singapore, the opportunity to "make overtime" would still make it possible to save money. However, the Gulf has some aspects that make it an attractive destination well, among which free work visas and accommodation with food. Yet as this agent was also keen to point out:

> There is no job and payment guarantee and they work for around [Rs.] 15k per month. Persons who don't find jobs to earn 15k per month in India prefer Gulf jobs. But in Singapore minimum amount of payment per month stands out around 30k and even up to 100,000 per month along with extra work and extra pay also possible since working on Sundays[6] and other public holidays provide double income.

Agency D was of the opinion that "within next 2-3 years the Gulf will overtake Singapore in jobs." He further added that "Recruitment for Singapore is tough. It is easier for the Gulf regions. Since migration rules are very strict in Singapore people prefer to go to Gulf." Agency K echoed this and argued that: "Overall job market for Singapore has come down and it may be caused with international trend." This agent in particularly also voiced his concerns over political developments in Singapore, especially with reference to anti-migrant sentiments (fueled by the Little India riots earlier).

Agency M was perhaps the most explicit in valuing the Gulf over Singapore as a migration destination, yet noting the advantages of Singapore over the Gulf as well:

> I get puzzled when there is an enquiry regarding migration to Singapore. Gulf in my personal opinion is better than Singapore. In Gulf they provide free accommodation. Food depending up on the company policy either they provide free meals or provide food coupons or provide kitchen and utensils alone. Here in Singapore once they were providing free food later it was changed. Then why they are going to Singapore means (1) Their relatives or friends may have referred (2) Cultural reasons, (3) For U turns Singapore pays more salary. In Singapore they start to earn around Rs. 25,000 per month. Later it increases. While they U turn little bit more and agents who sent them

---

[6]This appears to have changed recently. Sundays now only offer 1.5 pay while working on National Holidays continues to be awarded with double pay.

too charge lesser than the previous time. Singapore returnees here may earn up to a lakh maximum per month. It also depends on cadre and other things.

Comparing migration destinations thus adds further insight into what contributes to or is included in the costing of migration. Cultural closeness, brand value, and better migrant worker rights and protection all appear to be variables that make Singapore relatively more expensive than migration destinations in the Middle East. At the same time, such comparisons also underline that it is almost impossible to derive at a clear cut understanding of what contributes precisely to the factor cost when it comes to low-skilled migration from Tamil Nadu to Singapore. Migration agents also often contradict themselves and each other here. Except for one agent who had been a migrant in Singapore himself, none of the other agents I interviewed had ever been to Singapore or the Middle East. As much as they often sought to assure me that migrant wellbeing was something they genuinely cared for, in the end what mattered to them the most was how many migrants they would be able to send to a particular destination and, of course, the "cut" they would be able to make per migrant. As one informant underlined it during a discussion: "For us it's a business. We care for the migrants but we are here to make the money."

Conclusion

As was noted in the introduction, the factor of money is crucial in understanding the trajectories of low-skilled migrants. First of all, it should be clear that migration tends to cost more the lower skilled a particular migrant is. Migration to Singapore is not possible for low-skilled migrants without the assistance of at least a license holding agent. At the time of research, the deposit required to be licensed was Rs. 10 lakhs, a prohibitive amount for smaller players. At the time, the rumor was that this amount would soon be increased to thirty if not fifty lakhs. While part of the reasoning behind raising this amount is a genuine concern for migrant workers abroad, it cannot be denied that the cost for this "protection" will be borne by the migrants themselves. At the time of research, the "cut" a license holder would take was generally Rs. 10,000 but it is safe to assume that this will increase as a result. The mandatory involvement of a Singaporean counterpart—who is entitled to double the amount the Indian-based agent is (thus basically the equivalent of two months' worth of salary)—further adds to making Singapore a particularly pricey destination compared to the Gulf,

Middle East or even Malaysia. At the same time, Singapore continues to be popular due to its cultural closeness, climate, and generally perceived living conditions.

I argue that opening the black box of migration should revolve around thinking through the puzzle as outlined above. Migration equals money; it costs to migrate, while the objective to migrate tends to be money-driven. In another publication (Baas 2017), I discussed how migrants (former Work Pass and now S Pass holders) had used their savings to make investments in property in Tamil Nadu. Ostensibly positive accounts of upward visa and socioeconomic mobility, their narrations contrast with a more generally held perception that many migrant workers in Singapore struggle to make ends meet. At the same time, their trajectories were equally revealing for the exploitation and issues of non-pay migrant workers frequently face as well.

While the involvement of migrant agents is frequently pointed at to underline the financial precarious situation many migrant workers are in, what remains understudied is how the amounts charged are calculated. This chapter should be thought of as an attempt to provide more insight into this; not so much to de-vilify agents or brokers but to demystify a particular conundrum in migration research, the way migration actually functions (as a business or industry). With the ongoing commercialization of migration pathways, a much more structural focus should be on how the various components that make up and facilitate migration "add up." An important question that should be integral to the investigation is how protective measures, government interventions, and other types of interference contribute to the cumulative costing of migration. I argue that this will contribute to improving the chances, livelihoods, and futures of migrant workers in destinations across the globe.

REFERENCES

Baas, M. (2017). The mobile middle: Indian skilled migrants in Singapore and the 'middling' space in-between migration categories. *Transitions: Journal of Transient Migration, 1*(1), 47–63.

Goh, C., Wee, K., & Yeoh, B. S. A. (2016). *Who's holding the bomb? Debt-financed migration in Singapore's domestic work industry* (Working paper 38). Migrating out of Poverty.

Lindquist, J. (2010). Labour recruitment, circuits of capital and gendered mobility: Reconceptualizing the Indonesia migration industry. *Pacific Affairs, 83*(1), 115–132.

Lindquist, J., Xiang, B., & Yeoh, B. S. A. (2010). Introduction: Opening the black box of migration: Brokers, the organization of transnational mobility and the changing political economy in Asia. *Pacific Affairs, 83*(1), 7–19.

Rahman, M. D. M. (2017). *Bangladeshi migration to Singapore: A process-oriented approach.* Singapore: Springer.

CHAPTER 5

Unauthorized Recruitment of Migrant Domestic Workers from India to the Middle East: Interest Conflicts, Patriarchal Nationalism and State Policy

Praveena Kodoth

Introduction

The recruitment of women domestic workers from South India for employment in the Middle East has been consigned to an underbelly of the recruitment industry, animated by unauthorized agents and irregular practices and is mired in disrepute. Most women who seek jobs as domestic workers hold Emigration Check Required (ECR) passports, specially designated for people with less than a stipulated level of education at present those who have not completed class 10.[1] The ECR category was devised to protect a class

---

[1] Emigration check is mandated for workers going to eighteen countries which include all of the Middle East. People with the requisite education are categorized as Emigration Check Not Required (ECNR). It was announced on January 13, 2018, that henceforth ECR passports would come in orange jackets and hence be more distinct.

P. Kodoth (✉)
Centre for Development Studies, Thiruvananthapuram, India
e-mail: praveena@cds.ac.in

of unskilled workers but the promise of protection is rendered weak as it relies merely on verification of a prescribed set of documents (Kodoth and Varghese 2011; Varghese this volume). The recruitment of women in the ECR category differs from that of men in significant respects. At present, women domestic workers may be recruited through only specified state owned recruiting agencies and are required to produce for scrutiny before the Protector of Emigrants (POE), the office that is authorized to grant emigration clearance, evidence that they are between 30 and 50 years of age, a valid work contract and visa. Migrants in the ECR category are rarely accompanied by family members but women's mobility independent of their families flouts patriarchal social norms and is coded in sexual terms.

Regulatory regimes that seek to control migration divert aspirants to the use of irregular and often hazardous routes (for a recent review, see Fernandez 2012). But gendered restrictions have generated fears that the state is intent upon denying women's aspirations and has bred a complex nexus between emigrant women and unauthorized agents. With considerable profits to be reaped, recruiters are proactive in mobilizing clients even in the face of stringent controls. Unauthorized recruiters are well organized and believed to be effective hence even workers who source visas through kin or social networks seek out their assistance to comply with emigration check procedures.

Despite the characterization of migration to the Middle East as inherently temporary, the temporal depth of migration has structured a transnational community marked by continuous exchanges across the border and generational reproduction of ties. Transnational communities with strong stakes in mobility have powerful motivation to overcome barriers imposed by states (Castles 2004). Specific regions in South India have strong transnational ties that condition the recruitment of domestic workers. Migrant families and kin clusters but also recruiters who are drawn from among migrants and operate on either side of the border in a way that is often seamless with migrants nurturing transnational ties assiduously.

The failure to see migration as a social process undermines an understanding of the complex motivations of actors involved as well as the significance of connections and networks that assist migration. Scholars have pointed out that state policies may affect migration but they do not drive or necessarily control the migration process. Castles (2004, 858) explains that 'regulatory failure' is produced by the economic and bureaucratic rationale of state centric analysis which assumes that 'migration can be turned on and off like a tap by appropriate policy settings'. The standard approach expects that regulation of intermediaries will lead to better coordination of labour markets, curb irregular migration and afford greater protection for migrants but when regulation fails to achieve these objectives, the terms of the analysis limit the explanation to either the lack of adequate laws or poor implementation (Fernandez 2012, 817).

Unauthorized recruitment may be explained better through a decentred approach that shifts the analytical focus from the state and to what escapes regulation, which allows us to examine both how regulation works and why it may fail. Because knowledge and power are fragmented and because actors and systems have a certain autonomy (or are 'ungovernable') 'regulation may seek to modify actions, but its outcomes are contingent on the differential power of multiple actors, their susceptibility to regulatory intervention, and their attitudes toward compliance' (Fernandez 2012, 816).

Migrant Domestic Workers from India

Domestic workers from India are recruited in an opaque regulatory environment marked by a tough rhetoric of protection, frequent changes in legal requirements and significant irregular mobility. Legal barriers speak directly to dominant patriarchal and nationalist logics that represent control over women's bodies as normative but there is also a tacit acceptance of unauthorized recruitment. Castles (2004, 867) points out policy makers may be unable to ignore nationalist and ethnocentric ideologies implicit in public opinion but their interventions are not designed to comply with them either. The regulatory environment in India embeds the struggle to represent the contentious demands of powerful interest groups. As a result, state policy speaks in different and contrary voices.

In 2015, India adopted measures to stop recruitment to Kuwait, hitherto the largest receiving destination of Indian domestic workers with strong transnational ties with sending regions in India. The avowed position of the state has been to discourage recruitment, but in 2014, India signed a first of its kind agreement with Saudi Arabia to facilitate the mobility of domestic workers. Saudi Arabia suffers from significant shortages of domestic workers and Saudi contractors are reported to be pressurizing Indian recruiters to supply domestic workers in return for other contracts. Saudi Arabia has the worst record of protecting workers' rights in the Middle East, and despite sabre rattling by the Indian government in response to highly publicized cases of abuse, recruitment continues unabated in less than transparent circumstances. Emigrant domestic workers are drawn from marginal sections of Indian society and have little voice in public policy debates that most concerns them.[2] An interventionist state claims to speak 'in their interests' and 'for their protection', but it bears asking: In practice are not domestic workers being reduced to pawns in the struggle among powerful and competing interest?

Unauthorized recruitment is at least partially a legacy of a regulatory vacuum that marked the three decades following independence in 1947. While gendered controls may have expanded the scale of unauthorized brokerage since the 1980s, this chapter argues that a mobility agreement alongside intensification of controls in the recent past has given impetus to a specific type of brokerage that is clandestine and poses new uncertainties for workers. India's policy of curbing the recruitment of domestic workers has been interpreted in different ways. Pattadath and Moors (2012, 152) have argued that state actors misrecognize the problems of domestic workers and instead of helping to solve them may well be putting them in a more insecure position. Another view has been that a policy of restrictions serves the interests of unorganized recruiters and rent-seeking state officials (Kodoth and Varghese 2011). Recent interventions consolidate the grounds to believe that the state concedes regulatory 'gaps' as it is forced to negotiate the demands of multiple interest groups.

This chapter draws on material generated through fieldwork in the Godavari delta and Kadapa in Andhra Pradesh and Trivandrum and Malappuram districts in Kerala. In 2013, I conducted a sample survey of 500 emigrant women domestic workers (women who had returned not earlier than 2008) and interviews with domestic workers, their family members, recruiting agents and civil society activists engaged in repatriation of workers. This was followed up between 2014 and 2017, with interviews in Trivandrum with women who had migrated prior to 1970 and/or their family members and with returnee women or family members of emigrants to probe specific cases of ongoing migration.

The chapter is organized in five sections. In the Section "Overview of Recruitment", the transformation of recruitment of domestic workers is

---

[2] Emigrant domestic workers are mostly from the socially disadvantaged groups, the Scheduled Castes (SCs) who were historically oppressed and are listed in the first schedule of the Constitution, and the Other Backward Classes (OBC) who are described under the Constitution as 'socially and educationally backward classes'. In my sample survey, domestic workers from Kerala were overwhelmingly from the OBC (Latin Catholic, Muslim and Hindu) (82%) followed by SC (10%) whereas from AP they comprised 47% each from SC and OBC.

discussed as a response to two sets of factors—the huge expansion of demand in the Middle East and policy changes in India. The following section provides an overview of policy changes with respect to women's recruitment from India. Section "Indian State Policy" probes interest conflicts as they are expressed in the regulation of the recruitment of domestic workers to the Middle East. The Section on "Interest Conflict" then examines recent experiences of women recruited to Kuwait and Saudi Arabia and brings into view the problem of clandestine recruitment.

Overview of Recruitment

The recruitment of women domestic workers in the present may be delineated with reference to three contextual features. First, the regulatory regime which has evolved in three distinct phases, an initial phase (1950–1983) of continuity with the late colonial period which was characterized by lax regulation, followed by a phase (1983–2000) of sporadic restrictions coeval with emergent construction of emigrant domestic workers as a social problem and the current phase (2000–the present) of stringent restrictions on women's mobility. Second, the striking differences in the perspectives of policy makers and sending communities/families which place legal restrictions in a state of tension with the aspirations of workers. Third, transnational communities that are at ease with mobility and in possession of strong networks and connections that spur mobility aspirations.

The Early Phase

The 1940s saw the beginning of an organized flow of South Indian women to the Middle East, first as nurses and soon after in less skilled jobs prominently domestic work.[3] The woman who is remembered to have initiated migration from a coastal village in Trivandrum known as 'Kochu Kuwait' or 'little Kuwait' (because of its high density of women migrants) went to Kuwait to work for the family of the sister of the local parish priest in 1955.[4] Migration of the first generation of domestic workers was embedded in

---

[3] In the 1930s, the British imported a small number of South Asians to manage oil exploitation in the Middle East, marking the beginning of the modern era of labour migration to the region (Errichiello 2012, 399).

[4] This account is abstracted from interview with the early cohort of migrants from Trivandrum and East Godavari. For details, see (Kodoth 2016b). Information about the earliest

family connections that were respected.[5] Kin connections were critical in enabling access to visas to the early cohort of women migrants but the assistance of recruiters was indispensable for obtaining the documentation that was necessary for emigration.

Brokers played a more extensive role in East Godavari connecting the early cohort of women to agencies in Bombay (now Mumbai) that supplied them with visas. Bombay was the recruiting hub for employment in the Middle East. It housed the offices of the large recruitment agencies and had facilities to shelter workers for periods that could go up to several months. In the 1970s and 1980s, agents channelled large numbers of aspiring migrants to the city with the promise of getting them visas. Lakshmi who was an agricultural labourer in East Godavari before she obtained a visa to Kuwait in 1971 provides a glimpse of the recruiting process.

> There was one agent from this area, he used to take people and put them in touch with another agent from Kadapa named Syed Moosa. He was a big agent. He used to take the people from Bombay to the ship. He used to do the passport and visa related work… I heard that he [the former agent] had taken some women mainly from the Sakhinettipalli area. Then we thought that as we are poor, if we go to Kuwait we can earn some money and can feed the children… My mother's sister was in Sakhinettipalli. She took me to the agent and introduced me. He asked for some photos and papers, then we submitted them and then he took some of us to Bombay.

Muslim traders from Kadapa and the Malabar region (of Kerala) had connections with Arab businessmen who visited Bombay. These connections provided the base for a mode of recruitment through a chain of intermediaries that networked the sending regions with Bombay. People from the sending regions had moved to Bombay in search of work during the colonial period, and these connections too came in handy.[6] Aspirants drew

emigrant domestic who went in 1955 from Trivandrum is sourced from her daughter and other family members.

[5] The early migrants from Trivandrum ranged from housewives from comparatively well to do fisher families (that owned their own fishing boats) to poor mostly self-employed women. For a more detailed account of the early phase of migration from the Trivandrum coast in Kerala, see Kodoth (2016b). The first generation of women emigrants from East Godavari was more heterogeneous, including school teachers from families that faced downward mobility, agricultural labourers, manufacturing workers and housewives.

[6] People from the coastal villages in Trivandrum and from East Godavari were employed in Bombay in lower level government jobs and in the expansive informal sector. I learnt that small

upon family members and acquaintances in Bombay to get information about jobs, for logistical support and financial assistance.

> In 1970, Lalitha an agricultural labourer from East Godavari was too poor to raise the money required for the emigration expenses to Kuwait. Her cousin who worked in a 'pen factory' in Bombay helped her raise money. Some of the early emigrants had prior acquaintance with Bombay. Beatrice who went to Kuwait in 1968 used to transport small quantities of red rice from mills in Travancore for sale to Malayalee families in the city when inter-state movement of rice was banned due to scarcity. Beatrice's sister made a living in Bombay selling illicit liquor.

Migration largely to the Middle East and to the West occurred broadly under the purview of Emigration Act, 1922, but attracted little attention from the newly formed Indian state until three decades after independence (Nair 1998, 274).[7] The new Emigration Act, 1983, sought to regulate an established system of recruitment. The key features of the new legislation were the emigration check mechanism for migrants with ECR passports and the introduction of licensing for recruitment agents. The emigration check mechanism provided a means for the state to assert control over unskilled workers while more educated/skilled workers were free of such scrutiny. The licensing requirement redefined smaller brokers and subagents as unauthorized actors.

The early 1980s also saw the inception of migration controls targeted specifically at women. Lalitha recalled Indira Gandhi's visit to Kuwait and the subsequent ban on women's recruitment from India:

> During that time Indira Gandhi came to Kuwait. She said my Indian people in Kuwait are facing problems they are in jail and all that; 'when the women

entrepreneurs from East Godavari who had established pen manufacturing units in Bombay mobilized a large number of children from poor families in the villages to work in these units.

[7] The 1922 legislation was enacted by the British government in the face of strident criticism against indentured labour migration.

working there come back to India don't send them to Kuwait again'. She passed that order. My employers thought of taking a ticket to send me to India during the next month. At that time my sisters [female relatives] and other known people came from India, they said that they are taking the passport [not giving permission to leave the country]. We got letters from India not to come at this time…

Her words encapsulate the instinctive urge of the sending community to protect migrant employment against a patriarchal state that sought to exercise control over women.[8]

Unauthorized Brokerage

Expanding demand for domestic workers in the Middle East in the 1980s provided impetus for proactive recruitment and was accompanied by persistent reports of abuse, which contributed to the construction of women's migration as a social problem. Patriarchal and caste norms intersected with the nature of domestic work and spawned pejorative perceptions of emigrant domestic workers. Because women's mobility independent of their families is associated with loss of sexual control, these perceptions are framed in terms of a social and sexual binary.[9] Women were seen either as too 'timid' to cope with conditions in the Middle East and therefore susceptible to sexual and other forms of exploitation or as unscrupulous and hence not unwilling to engage in sexually permissive behaviour for illicit gains.

The social construction of women emigrants as a problem has been drawn into the regulation of recruitment. Public sector recruiting agencies steadfastly refused to recruit domestic workers. Officials of these agencies claimed that such recruitment would go against the grain of a sexually conservative 'society' like India and would only sully their image.[10] Licensed recruiters in the private sector too expressed reluctance to recruit women

---

[8] There were protests against this apparently from Goan and Malayalee families and 'Indian officials *quietly* permitted resumption of the migration' (Weiner 2007, emphasis added).

[9] Within the caste order, groups at the lower end of the hierarchy are considered sexually permissive and women of the socially privileged castes are subject to rigid sexual controls.

[10] Interactions with officials of public sector overseas recruiting agencies in Kerala. An official of a public sector recruiting agency in undivided AP said an initiative towards training and recruiting domestic workers had run into political roadblocks. See also Walton Roberts (2012, 186).

workers for similar reasons but they also underlined their own vulnerability in the existing regulatory environment. A representative of the private recruiting agents in Andhra Pradesh explained that women clients lacked training and preparedness to cope with conditions in the Middle East, but under the current system when women made formal complaints of mistreatment, recruiters were held responsible and could lose their licenses.[11] According to him, even recruiters who played by the rules feared that it was too big a risk to recruit women as domestic workers.

However, it is not conclusively apparent that licensed recruiters do not recruit women in this segment. The sole licensed recruiter in a Kadapa town said that he had stopped recruiting domestic workers in the 1980s, but some of the domestic workers I interviewed said that they had been recruited through this agency.[12] Unauthorized agents in the same town claimed that this licensed recruiter used his legal status to extract a higher price from clients. Thus, legal controls may have generated perverse incentives to extort a price from workers and to recruit through irregular channels.[13]

In the unauthorized segment of the recruiting industry are a range of actors including travel agents, recruiting networks operating on either side of the border and independent brokers. Intervention by unauthorized agents did not necessarily mean that migrants left the country through the irregular channel. Unauthorized agents provided visas to workers and assisted them with emigration procedures or did only the latter where migrants had obtained visas independently. In these circumstances, migrants obtained emigration clearance and left the country through the legal route. It is only when they are unable to obtain emigration clearance that emigrant workers leave the country illegally.

Unauthorized agents too underlined the difficulties associated with recruiting women in the ECR segment. Abdulla who had a travel and tour agency in the Kadapa town maintained that recruitment of domestic

---

[11] Conversation with the President of the AP private recruiting agents' association in Vijayawada in December 2016. A group of travel agents in Kadapa echoed the same view in a conversation in November 2013.

[12] Interviews in November 2013.

[13] Less than five per cent of intending migrant domestics surveyed at the seven offices of the POE across India were recruited by licensed recruiting agencies and less than 10% of licensed recruiting agents surveyed from across the country said that they recruited domestic workers (Rajan et al. 2011).

workers was a messy business. As I spoke to Abdulla at his travel agency, several agents gathered around and chipped in with their experiences. All of them has worked in the Middle East and had turned to the recruiting business on their return. They sought to counter the dominant narrative about recruiters being exploitative by presenting emigrant women in terms of the social and sexual binary. According to them, emigrant women got into trouble when they sought out illicit freedoms but were safe when they conformed to the rules. They maintained that a small proportion of women 'brought a bad name' by 'running away' from their sponsors and entering into illicit relationships in the destination. Abdulla explained that recruiters were compensated for the expenses incurred on sending women overseas only after the workers were placed in employment. If a woman ran away from her sponsor during the initial period of employment, the recruiting agent would lose the entire investment. Similar views were expressed by travel agents in Trivandrum.[14]

Under the Kafala system of sponsorship and recruitment followed in the Middle East, it is mandatory for sponsors to pay the expenses of recruitment and emigration of migrant workers. This amount is released to the recruiters in India only after the workers in placed in employment in the destination. However, recruiters suffer losses (if a woman runs away) only when they actually pay for the worker's recruitment. In most cases, domestic workers reported paying for their own emigration. Recruiters siphon off the money paid by the sponsor for the worker's emigration systematically by making the worker pay these costs.

Recruiters operating under the banner of travel agencies obtained visas directly from sponsors in the Middle East using their connections or from recruiting agencies of varied legal status in the destination.[15] Most of the unauthorized recruiters I spoke to had nurtured connections with sponsors and/or with recruiting agencies in the Middle East.[16] A recruiter who was based in Kuwait, who I spoke to in East Godavari, said he sourced visas

---

[14] One of these agents had recruited women workers for many years but his license had been suspended after he was embroiled in a legal case which according to him was the result of professional jealousy.

[15] Domestic workers, who were recruited by travel agents at home, were in some instances received directly by the sponsor at the airport and in others received by agents and either made to wait at the offices of recruiting agencies till a sponsor was found for them or registered at the agency office and claimed immediately by a sponsor.

[16] Interviews with travel agents in Kadapa, East Godavari, Trivandrum and Malappuram.

directly from sponsors in Kuwait and supplied them to recruiters in East Godavari and Kadapa. His wife had worked in Kuwait as a domestic worker. Formally, he held a driver's visa but had an arrangement with his sponsor that allowed him to work independently. Migrant workers in the Middle East are legally bound to work exclusively for their sponsors; hence, it is illegal to be self-employed or to work for employers who are not sponsors. But visas may be purchased at a hefty price from sponsors directly or through agents. These are popularly referred to as 'free' or *azad* visas. Workers on free visas look for work on a thriving but illegal open market.

Transnational 'Family' Ties

Strong transnational ties are evident in the ease of access to visas in the sending regions. Emigrant women from Trivandrum frequently sourced visas from travel agents, and they believed visas could be procured from almost any travel agent. Information about jobs in the Middle East circulated widely in the villages of the sending regions and agents could be contacted with almost alarming ease. Mumtaz, who lived in an interior village in Kadapa, was barely 15 years old in 2001 when she went to Kuwait for the first time. She was encouraged by the local people to go because her parents were too poor to arrange her marriage. 'They used to tell me about the agent, that if you pay Rs. 30,000 he will send you'. Brokers were household names in specific localities as they used kin and spatial connections to mobilize workers.

In June 2013, an emigrant domestic worker from East Godavari had returned from Oman after her employer failed to pay her salary for the first three months of employment. In September 2013, when I went to meet her, her husband, Mohan, said that it was a month since she had left for Kuwait.[17] In the four months preceding my meeting with Mohan, his mother too had returned from Oman and left for Abu Dhabi. The family had sourced successive visas for Mohan's wife and mother from local unauthorized agents. In this family, Mohan's sister was the only female member still residing in the village as his elder brother's wife too was a domestic worker but in Bahrain.

However, women's accounts suggest that channels of migration are differentiated. The route considered safest was through a visa obtained from

[17] Interview, East Godavari, September 2013.

one's own kin. A frequently expressed distinction was between 'office' visas and 'agent' visas. Women used the term 'office' visas to refer to visas that were sourced from recruiting agencies in the destination. Women would explain that agents or sponsors who received them on arrival in the destination took them to the office of the recruiting agency in the destination to complete formalities of sponsorship. A few of the respondents said they had waited at the office for periods ranging from a few days to two months before they found a sponsor.[18] By 'agent' visas, workers referred to visas that were sourced through independent agents or informal networks.

> Sita had two decades of experience in the Middle East as a domestic worker. Towards the end of an extended conversation at her home in East Godavari, she inquired whether we knew any women who would be interested in obtaining visas (to work as domestic workers in Oman).[19] She revealed that a visa would cost Rs. 30,000 but the client would have to 'do her own emigration', referring to the emigration clearance procedure. Sita had developed sufficient contacts with employers in the Middle East to act as a small-time independent broker. Initially, she had concealed the fact that she was on a 'free' visa. This became apparent when I asked her whether her employer troubled her. She responded 'how can she do that when I am on my own visa?' However, access to 'free' visas was contingent on strong networks in the destination or personal connections developed over a period of time. In 2013, Sita earned Rs. 20,000 a month as a full-time domestic worker for an Arab family. Recruitment of a single worker could fetch a substantial profit for Sita.

[18] Sponsors and workers could seek a change but workers rarely were able to use this because they could be prevented.

[19] Interview, East Godavari, December 2013. At the time, Sita was working in Oman but had worked previously in Saudi Arabia and Kuwait.

Issues of Abuse and Exploitation

Emigrant women become aware of the complications of going through unauthorized recruiters upon reaching the destination. Under the sponsorship system, workers must be placed with a sponsor within three months of arrival in the destination and have their *iquama* (residence permit) stamped. As their profits depend on ensuring successful placement of workers, recruiters may exploit their position as the only connection that workers have in the destination or contrive to isolate workers from the outside world in order to force them to remain with a sponsor even when the latter is abusive or fails to pay wages in part or full. However, women's experiences varied. Kafala rules mandate that workers cannot change a sponsor after the residence permit is made but agents had assisted women who were in distress to find new employers even after the lapse of three months.

The most unscrupulous actors are independent recruiting networks (comprising brokers from Kerala and AP) that supply workers to sponsors at the lowest end of the market. These networks are run by two or three individuals and operate in ways that fosters uncertainty.

> In 2012, Florence sourced a visa to the UAE from a broker in her village in East Godavari and was received on arrival in Abu Dhabi by his associate, a Telugu-speaking woman. The 'office' of this network was located on the UAE–Oman border at Al Ain. After two months, the woman associate left the country forcing Florence to take up a job across the border in Oman. Her Omani sponsor failed to pay her salary regularly but matters came to a head after 11 months when a child entrusted to her care got hurt. Florence said the 'mama' (the woman employer/sponsor or the wife of the male sponsor) had accused her of negligence and brandished a knife at her. She believed that the lady was threatening to kill her and ran away to the Indian Embassy.

Recruiters seek to make quick profits and are eager to ensure that workers comply with the demands of employers. Women's experiences suggest that sponsors undercut wages and burden workers with excessive work at least partially to compensate for the large amounts they pay to recruiters. To secure their profits, recruiters may collude with abusive sponsors and may bring pressure on workers to comply with excessive demands.[20]

Emigration Services

Some of the brokers drew a fine distinction between 'recruitment' or the provision of visas and 'emigration services' or assistance rendered to migrants with the procedures for getting emigration clearance.[21] Abdulla insisted that he did not recruit women but only provided assistance with emigration procedures. He showed me a copy of the work contract and passport of a woman domestic worker in his possession saying that she had approached him after getting a visa.[22] Brokers in the Kadapa town had set up a well-coordinated network of services for their clients. There were regular taxi services on specific days every week from this town to the nearest centres for police clearance, medical clearance and emigration clearance. A taxi driver who was a return migrant from Saudi Arabia had been hired by a group of travel agents to take their clients to Hyderabad twice every week where he also guided the aspirants through the process of emigration clearance.[23] In East Godavari, brokers accompanied groups of aspirants to Hyderabad for emigration clearance or deputed a person to accompany and guide them. There was also a direct bus to Shamshabad airport in Hyderabad.

Migration controls gave a particular salience to unauthorized brokerage. The minimum age for women emigrants was flouted rampantly. My sample survey showed that 42.6% of workers who took up their first overseas jobs after 2000 were below 30 years at the time of migration.[24] Unauthorized agents are deft at manipulating emigration procedures. Women who do not qualify for emigration clearance could go through 'pushing', by bribing the concerned emigration officials at airports. Abdullah and the agents who had

---

[20] For analysis of cases, see Kodoth (2016c).

[21] Discussion with travel agents in Kadapa, November 2013.

[22] Discussion with a group of travel agents and informal recruiting agents in Rayachoty, November 2013.

[23] The taxi service I had hired had sent this taxi driver on the days he was in Kadapa.

[24] More than half the workers in my sample (307) had migrated since 2000. About 53% of all workers were below 30 years at the time of their first journey.

gathered in his office explained that pushing works like a chain. Emigration officials are identified through the agents' network and the passport details of candidates are passed on them. Money changes hands. 'There are many high profile people involved in this pushing to get illegal income. It involves IAS officers and other government officers from different departments'. At the time of the interview, women were being sent through pushing from Delhi, Pune and Lucknow. Three days prior to the interview, they had stopped using Hyderabad. Abdullah explained, 'when an officer comes from outside, the existing officer will get scared and stops doing this work. He communicates to us not to send the persons for pushing as the work has been stopped. Then we look at other options like Delhi'.

> Vasanta, a broker based in her village in East Godavari, claimed that she had accompanied her clients to airports across the country, 'Hyderabad, Madras, Delhi, Kerala, Bangalore etc., where ever the flight is from'. Agents source information from the official who 'sets up' pushing. 'The "setting" person will ask us to come saying he is in an airport in Kerala, then we take all the people and go there. For example, I will take four persons, another agent will get four persons and like that the agents we go together to the airport'.

> Rama, who had returned from Muscat where she had worked as a domestic worker described the circumstances in which she went through pushing in 2006. 'First I went to Madras. I didn't know anything. I was assisted by relatives of my paternal uncle… I didn't have the agreement [work contract] that is why I went through pushing from Madras. The second time I went from Hyderabad by myself and got emigration'.

When I visited the POE's office on three occasions in 2013, women were required to go in person to get emigration clearance as the rules prevented recruiting agents from representing them. There were long queues of women (100 or more) each time waiting for emigration clearance, and it was immediately apparent that they were accompanied by an assortment of men including recruiting agents, subagents or relatives. But recruiting agents organized the visit of aspiring migrants to the POE offices and guided them through the process. In the late afternoon just before the POE met and counselled the women applicants, agents could be seen speaking to women in small groups and distributing papers to them. On one occasion, I was approached by a tout who asked whether I was interested in obtaining a visa domestic workers. He said he was from a village in East Godavari and his wife who had returned from the UAE after eight years could arrange for a visa.

Unauthorized agents also assist aspiring women get documents based on false information. Rama was only 18 years old when she left for Oman in 2006, but her passport which was made that year showed her age as 30 years. To overstate her age on her passport, Rama's broker procured a certificate from the local authorities attesting to a false date of birth. It is the practice to use school leaving certificates as proof of age in applications for passports. Because it is not possible to alter the school-leaving certificate, women are certified as illiterate and birth certificates with a false date of birth are obtained. When they are recruited through unauthorized brokers, aspirants may not be able to obtain work contracts, which are necessary for emigration clearance.

Rama had dropped out of school to take up daily wage labour and help her mother, who was a single parent of failing health. She earned a mere Rs. 50 a day in East Godavari in 2006, and work was not assured when she decided to go to Oman. As a domestic worker in Oman, she earned Rs. 4500 a month. The expenses incurred on 'emigration services' ranged from anywhere between Rs. 30,000 ($500) and Rs. 70,000 ($1200) and, because of the nature of unauthorized recruitment, variations could be quite arbitrary. Rama paid Rs. 35,000 for her visa and other expenses on her first journey. Women expect regular jobs with relatively higher remuneration in the Middle East and are willing to borrow from local moneylenders at high interest rates to pay these costs.

INDIAN STATE POLICY

Successive Indian governments have imposed restrictions against women workers on ECR passports. The POE grants 'emigration clearance' on the basis of verification of documents which include passports, visas and employment contracts. Since the 1990s, women below 30 years of age in the ECR category have been prohibited from taking up employment (Oishi and Lum 1996). The promise of protection relies entirely on preventing the departure of aspirants with improper documentation, and while it creates conditions for criminalization of women who go through irregular channels, it also legitimizes the lack of support to women workers in the destination.

The Protector General of Emigrants (PGE) under whom the POEs function is also responsible for the issue registration certificates to overseas recruitment agents. This office was attached to the Ministry of Labour until 2004, when emigration governance was brought under the newly formed Ministry of Overseas Indian Affairs (MOIA). Procedures for emigration checks have been reinforced since 2000 corresponding to greater public scrutiny of women's mobility in the face of increased flows of information. In 2002, the government reiterated the minimum age for women in the ECR category and justified it citing the recommendation of the National Women's Commission to extend it to all foreign countries in 2003. Women's advocates and even activist groups that intervene to 'rescue' women or seek to organize them are shy of vocally supporting women's migration as they too are invested in a dominant view that it is akin to 'sending women out to be exploited'.

In 2007, the ministry reviewed procedures again and mandated in August that year that prospective women emigrants produce a work contract stipulating a minimum monthly wage of $400 and a pre-paid mobile facility for the worker and attested by the Indian mission at the destination upon production by the sponsor of a bank guarantee of $2500 to facilitate repatriation of workers if the need arose. Soon after, however, it withdrew the stipulation of the minimum wage and the security deposit in September the same year on account of opposition from varied stakeholders.[25]

Recent measures have been directed at curbing the activities of private recruitment agents. The order passed in August 2007 required women domestic workers to have direct employment contracts between workers and employers suggesting that they were to be recruited directly and not

---

[25] For details of Government orders, see Kodoth and Varghese (2011).

through recruiting agents in India. Also, women were required to present themselves personally before the POE for emigration clearance; unlike men, they could no longer be represented by recruiting agents. These measures come in the wake of reports especially from aggrieved women that recruitment agents entice them with promises of employment and lead them into uncertain situations in the Middle East. Cases of abuse discussed in the media have highlighted cheating, trafficking and extortion by recruitment agents.

The MOIA ceased to exist in January 2016, when it was merged officially with the Ministry of External Affairs. The government claimed that this would provide the necessary human resources to give the office of the PGE 'a diplomatic focus' and therefore enable it 'to deal with emergencies involving Indians in various crisis-prone countries in West Asia'.[26] However, there was no change in the perspective that the solution to abuse of domestic workers in the Middle East lay in discouraging recruitment nor has there been any expansion in the infrastructure for the support of domestic workers in the destination countries.

In August 2016, the Indian government mandated that recruitment of 'female workers to the 18 ECR countries' would be done exclusively through specially notified state-owned recruiting agencies.[27] The order said that the action was taken in view of a reported increase in complaints of exploitation of women going to the 18 ECR countries and that all other instructions for the protection and welfare of women emigrants would continue. As discussed in the previous section, public sector agencies for overseas recruitment had no previous record of deployment of women domestic workers and had consistently expressed their aversion against such deployment, this move threatened to put a stop to the recruitment of domestic workers through the legal channel.

Even as the government was seen as signalling its resolve to suppress recruitment altogether it ceded ground again in small steps.[28] In September 2017, it did away with the bank guarantee 'for Employers recruiting

---

[26] Bhattacharya, K. (2017, January 7). Overseas Indian Affairs Ministry, MEA merged. *The Hindu*. It was reported that the merger was expected to 'increase efficiency of emergency work abroad'.

[27] Office Order NoZ-11025/126/2015-Emig (pt.File) of August 2, 2016.

[28] Kader (2016) and Chari (2016), Conversation with official of a public sector agency, December 2016.

female domestic workers from India through any of these 6 State Government Agencies', explaining that '[e]mployers of female domestic workers and Recruitment Agencies, have been pointing out that the financial guarantee... has been a key factor in discouraging recruitment of Indian female domestic workers through eMigrate system'.[29] But the Indian embassy in Oman indicated that a window was open to private operators, 'recruitment of Indian female domestic workers from *any other* Recruitment Agency in India will continue to require a bank guarantee of OMR 1100 and a NOC from the Embassy' (emphasis added, Embassy of India in Oman accessed on October 17, 2017).

Interest Conflict

Indian policy has vacillated between stringent curbs on domestic workers and contingent opening of doors to private operators. That conflicting pulls underpin this vacillation is evident from the reference by policy makers to the difficulties faced by recruiting agents and employers of domestics as reasons for partially rolling back the bank guarantee. However, a comparative perspective on India's recent policy level engagement with recruitment to Saudi Arabia and Kuwait suggests that there is a remarkably callous disregard for the interests of its emigrant domestic workers.

In January 2014, India and Saudi Arabia inked a domestic worker's mobility agreement (for men and women) and later that year the Saudi Labor Ministry announced plans to issue 100,000 visas for Indian domestic workers in 2015. The agreement constituted a sharp departure from India's hitherto emphasized position that it discouraged the recruitment of women domestics from India as the best means of preventing their abuse but was hailed as a step towards strengthening bilateral ties (Kodoth 2016a). Saudi Arabia finalized a standard contract for Indian domestic workers in December that year that included a commitment to enforcing the bank guarantee of $2500 to be submitted to the Indian embassy by sponsors of domestic workers. The contract by implication permits up to 16 hours of work a day and provides no guarantee of freedom of mobility and private access to communication. Also while it matches the Indian government's minimum wage requirement of $400, Saudi Arabia's record of enforcing previous minimum wages has been poor (migrantrights.org).

[29] Press Release, Embassy of India in Oman, September 18, 2017, see also notifications by the embassy of India in Kuwait and Saudi Arabia.

Saudi Arabia has the worst record on the protection of domestic workers in the Middle East. In September 2015, the Indian media was rife with reports of a South Indian domestic worker, Kasturi Munirathinam, who was severely injured in Saudi Arabia after a fall from the third floor of her employer's house and had her arm amputated as a result. Initial reports suggested that the worker's arm had been chopped off by her sponsor and fuelled public outrage.

'Alarmed by frequent allegations of sex slavery, arm-chopping and sadistic domestic torture of housemaids in Saudi Arabia, India is considering a total ban on recruitment of housemaids by that country. The idea of the ban was discussed by Ms. Swaraj [the foreign minister] at a meeting of the Parliamentary Consultative Committee of the Ministry of Overseas Indian Affairs (MOIA) and the Ministry of External Affairs on October 8. "Sushmaji and we discussed how to stop the flow of housemaids from Tamil Nadu's Vellore and West Godavari district of Andhra Pradesh, which top the list of regions producing housemaids for the Saudi kingdom", said Rajya Sabha member D. Raja, who is a member of the committee' (Bhattacharjee 2015). However, it became apparent also that domestic workers were being recruited in less than transparent circumstances. The Indian authorities blamed Saudi Arabia for 'facilitating an environment of impunity for Foreign Employers in Saudi territory who are forcing the recruitment agents of India to obey Saudi dictates neglecting Indian official procedures'.

'Saudi Arabia has refused to implement the $2500 bank guarantee that foreign employers are expected to deposit with the Embassy of India in Riyadh before approaching recruitment agents in India. More curiously, the Saudi authorities themselves have communicated to the Indian recruitment agents that they will be issued work visas only if they ensured that 25% of their total recruits are housemaids from India' (Bhattacharjee 2015). During the negotiation of the mobility agreement signed in 2014, Saudi Arabian contractors had insisted apparently on the supply of a specific proportion of women domestic workers in return for contracts for the supply of other workers and this was agreed upon implicitly.[30] Saudi Arabia was facing acute shortages of domestic workers as it had been black listed by its major suppliers, Indonesia, the Philippines and Ethiopia even as Indian business lobbies were pushing hard for expanding their interests in Saudi Arabia.

---

[30] This was revealed by a stakeholder who was privy to the negotiation.

Emigration Clearance and the Bank Guarantee

In 2013, when I conducted fieldwork in Andhra Pradesh and Kerala, Kuwait accounted for the bulk of emigration clearances granted to domestic workers. Kuwait had refused to accept India's $2500 bank guarantee condition for the supply of women domestic workers. The Indian government made it effective for recruitment to Kuwait in September 2014; i.e., it ceased to grant emigration clearance to domestic workers bound for Kuwait. In November 2015, India asked Kuwait to stop issuing visas to Indian domestic workers to stop illegal flows.[31] Kuwait is no exemplar on the protection of workers' rights, but migrant workers have greater freedom of mobility and informal association there than in Saudi Arabia. It is telling that despite weak enforcement of the bank guarantee condition and persistent reports of abuse that have highlighted complicity between recruitment agents and sponsoring employers, India has not stopped recruitment to Saudi Arabia.

Between 2012 and 2014, a disproportionately large proportion of emigration clearances granted to women were to Kuwait (Table 5.1).[32] In a small indication of how regulation works, Table 5.1 shows that within the steep overall decline in emigration clearances granted to women since 2014, emigration clearances to Saudi Arabia (minimal until 2014) showed a small increase in the two years following the bilateral agreement (Table 5.1).[33] Estimates of stock of Indian domestic workers from sources in the Middle East (that would include migration without emigration clearances or illegal

---

[31] Daniel, G. (2015). *Embassy of India, Kuwait.* http://www.indembkwt.org/dispnews.aspx?id=687&section=1, accessed on May 15, 2017.

[32] According to information sourced from the POE in Hyderabad, over 37,000 women were granted emigration clearance by his office alone and he estimated that over 90% of total emigration clearance granted to women was for Kuwait (Interview, February 22, 2013). See also Table 5.1 for 2013. Since the change in rules, the yard in front of the POE's office in Hyderabad which used to teem with women has almost emptied out. Observation by Sister Lizzy Joseph of the NDWM who conducted orientation sessions for women emigrants at the POE's office. Ironically, the re-routing of women through illegal channels makes them unavailable for these sessions.

[33] The number of Indian migrant domestic workers (male and female) who have been given emigration clearance for recruitment in gulf countries since September, 2014 till date is 58163. Unstarred Question no 3226, Rajya Sabha, Answered on December 15, 2016, Indian migrant domestic workers in the Gulf countries,

Table 5.1 Emigration clearances given to women from the top 25 sending districts from India, 2012–2017

	Kuwait	Oman	UAE	Saudi Arabia	Total ECR countries	From Godavari
2008	1251	4315	609	34	6352	4660
2009	4402	4659	735	52	9958	7549
2010	5808	1805	696	88	10,718	7906
2011	4387	3974	732	79	7042	4779
2012	6856	249	824	107	8094	5654
2013	8919	237	915	64	10,192	7537
2014	6793	204	859	7	7929	4874
2015	69	253	623	156	1167	99
2016	14	234	493	154	950	60
2017	0	127	402	51	631	34

Source eMigrate, Ministry of External Affairs

migration) suggest that there has been a steep increase in recruitment to Saudi Arabia in recent years.[34]

Recruiters and domestic workers from South India had nurtured social connections in Kuwait, Oman, Bahrain and the UAE riding on British oil interests in the region. Domestic workers from South India have continued to migrate using their networks despite the fact that an adverse policy regime has havoc on their reputation and labour market prospects in these countries (Kodoth 2016a).[35] Indian women workers' social networks were not as strong in Saudi Arabia as in Kuwait. And if Saudi Arabia has a notorious record of protection of the rights of women migrant workers, it also has a much less competitive labour market than Kuwait or the UAE. It is a compelling irony then that the government is now keen to offer domestic workers to Saudi Arabia. While the Indian state's intervention in banning

---

[34] Estimates of the stock of Indian women domestic workers in Saudi Arabia rose from 10,000 in 2001 to 50,000 in 2013 (Kodoth 2016a).

[35] In my sample survey, Kuwait accounted for 37% of journeys undertaken by sample domestic workers over varying periods of time and the UAE was the second most prominent destination. The sample was selected to reflect diversity of migrants and destinations and hence is likely to underestimate the dominant destinations and give relatively more prominence to less prevalent ones. Saudi Arabia accounted for 17% of journeys from Trivandrum and 12% from Kadapa, where it was second to Kuwait in terms of principal destinations (Kodoth 2016a). Other sources indicate that Kuwait and Oman are the largest destinations. For more detailed discussion, see Kodoth (2016a).

recruitment to Kuwait rather than intervening to protect workers' rights in that country brings to the fore its apathy towards the interests of emigrant domestics, its recent engagement with Saudi Arabia suggests a more scathing possibility that it is not unwilling to barter domestic workers to secure the interests of contractors and big business operating across India and Saudi Arabia.

CLANDESTINE RECRUITMENT AND CRIMINALIZATION OF WOMEN

I now take up two recent cases of recruitment to examine some of the effects of recent policy changes. My field work in Trivandrum suggests that women have continued to leave for Kuwait and to Saudi Arabia through 'pushing' or visit visas when sponsors refuse to observe the bank guarantee condition.[36] Once workers reach the Middle East, brokers may channel women across porous land borders as for instance between Kuwait and Saudi Arabia or between the UAE and Oman using their connections with immigration officials.[37]

Case 1

Reetha learnt of the possibility of employment in the Middle East through Alex, a pastor she met in church at her highland village in Trivandrum and was drawn to the idea because she wanted to raise money to build a house. She spoke about it to her brother, Laiju, who had been a construction worker in Saudi Arabia. Laiju met Alex and says the latter's manner and the way he spoke about Reetha's visa and emigration procedure made him suspicious so he advised Reetha against taking the offer. But Alex not only convinced her to go ahead with the plan but also to conceal information from Laiju and other people.

Three days before she was to leave home, Reetha announced to Laiju that she was leaving for Oman. He was shocked but decided to accompany

---

[36] Activists claim that domestic workers are routed through illegal channels including visit visas and evasion of emigration check. Employers are said to contact local agents or private recruitment agencies in order to avoid paying the bank guarantee (see Mallick 2017; Chari 2016).

[37] Interviews with women who had been taken across these international borders by the land route. See also Mallick (2017).

her to the airport. Alex had informed Reetha that she would fly out of Madurai, in Tamil Nadu. They took a train from Trivandrum but when they did not get off at Madurai, Laiju demanded an explantion but Alex refused to respond to his questions. It was clear that he was withholding information. They eventually got off the train at Nagpur in Maharashtra, and it was only at the airport when Alex gave Reetha her passport and ticket that Laiju saw that she was going on a visit visa to Kuwait (and not on a domestic work visa to Oman). Laiju says he was aware that emigration to Kuwait had been stopped but Reetha had made up her mind to go. Also she was not alone on the journey to Kuwait. At the airport, they met a number of other women who had been brought by their agents.

Reetha's troubles began as soon as she started to work for her sponsor. She did not know the language and had trouble adjusting. Her family in Trivandrum said that she complained of excessive work and constant scolding. It transpired that Alex had told Reetha that his wife worked in a hospital in Kuwait and would assist her but Reetha was not able to meet Alex's wife. On her arrival in Kuwait, a man called Reddy and his wife received and placed her in an Arab household. Three months elapsed and Reetha did not receive her salary. When her pleas to her agent in Kuwait were of no avail, she communicated her acute stress to her family.

In early 2016 in Trivandrum, a local newspaper reported that Reetha had gone 'missing' in Kuwait. By this time, Reetha had stopped communicating with her family. Seeing this, an activist from a women's organization contacted Laiju. With the support of the organization, Laiju approached an elected representative from the area who is from the Communist Party of India (Marxist) (henceforth CPI (M)) and also filed a case at the local police station but did not receive a response.[38] Laiju believed Alex was not revealing Reetha's whereabouts and that he was made bold by the protection he enjoyed from the local CPI (M). After much effort to contact people in Kuwait, the family learnt through a social worker in Kuwait that Reetha worked for a sponsor in a crime-infested area and that the laws in the country made it dangerous for them to try to contact her without a court order.

---

[38] Conversations with SEWA activists and with Reetha's brother and other family members at their home in May 2016.

Case 2

Michelle left for Saudi Arabia in September 2016 through 'pushing' from Ahmedabad in Gujarat. Her ECR category passport showed that she had a proper visa but she had not obtained emigration clearance from the POE.[39] Her sponsor did not provide an embassy attested work contract, which could be obtained only on payment of the bank guarantee. Michelle's agent, a man called Rajan, sourced visas from a recruiting agency in Dammam owned by an Arab and operated by a Malayalee man by the name Thomas. Michelle learnt about Rajan from two young women recruits from a coastal village in Trivandrum not far from her own. She only spoke to him over the phone and did not meet him. On Rajan's instructions, she handed over her passport and Rs. 80,000 for the visa and expenses to the two women. Sometime later, Michelle was surprised to learn from Rajan's associate in Trivandrum, a woman to whom she handed over her medical certificate (which was required for the visa) that Rajan did not have an office in Trivandrum. Michelle had worked for two years in Singapore in the late 1990s and was conscious of deception by recruiting agents. She says she asked the woman to return her passport only to be told that it had been sent to Bombay for the visa processing. Fearing that she may lose her passport and the money she had paid, she relented.

Michelle took a train to Bombay along with eight women all recruited by Rajan and bound for Saudi Arabia. Apart from the two young recruits of Michelle's acquaintance, the others were from different places in Kerala. In Bombay, Rajan's associate, a man called Nisar, met them and accompanied them to Ahmedabad.[40] Michelle and two other women left for Dammam on the day they reached Ahmedabad. At Dammam airport, a Saudi Arabian sponsor claimed Michelle. Rajan had assured her that the agency had arranged for her to live 'outside' in shared accommodation and that she could work in multiple part time jobs and earn SR 1200. So she protested and initially refused to go with the sponsor but they had papers with her photograph on it so she was compelled to go.

---

[39] Saudi Arabia provides a 90-day visa initially, and this is converted into a two-year work visa once a sponsor is found.

[40] Michelle first said she took the flight from Bombay but also that it took four days to reach the city which was unlikely. On examining her passport, I learnt that she had gone from Ahmedabad and have pieced together the account from her description.

Michelle's sponsor lived in a large house with three floors. As the sole worker, she was assigned all the cleaning. The sponsor's family gave her little food, and she felt dizzy often felt Unable to work, Michelle says she started to steal food but matters came to a head when the sponsor failed to pay her salary. Michelle refused to work, and the sponsor took her back to the agency, where Thomas tried to force her to return to the sponsor. When persuasion failed, he grew violent and injured Michelle's shoulder. Michelle wanted to go back home but a woman helper at the agency persuaded her to take up another job. For a few days, she worked in the house of the Arab owner of agency where she says she did not face problems but was forced to return to her earlier sponsor. Five months of back breaking work and no move by her sponsor to pay her, Michelle says she was in terrible distress. One of the two young recruits from Trivandrum who managed to contact her, advised her to run away to the Indian embassy. She succeeded in doing this at the first opportunity that presented itself. But she lost all her belongings because she threw the bundle at her employer when the latter tried to stop her. Running away is a criminal act; hence, Michelle was taken from the embassy to the police station and detained there before being allowed to go to the shelter. Michelle said 'social workers' visit the shelter to assist distressed workers in various ways. A social worker named Manju befriended Michelle. After about a month, Manju informed Michelle that she would soon be able to go home because her sponsor had agreed to return her travel documents and to pay for her ticket. Michelle had to meet her sponsor one final time in the presence of the embassy authorities. Just as she was called for the meeting, Manju warned her against going back to work for the sponsor. 'If you agree to go back the sponsor may kill you', Michelle recalled her saying.

Michelle was 'released' by the sponsor and scheduled to leave the country the following day. The shelter allowed Manju to take her home and to drop her at the airport the next day. At her home, Manju told Michelle that she could stay on in the country and work with Malayalee families. But when Michelle was not persuaded, Manju tried to brow beat her. That night, in considerable tension and uncertainty, Michelle learnt from another woman in the house that Manju and her husband 'operated a business' that channelled workers like them from the shelter back into jobs. On the day she was to leave, Manju was on the phone with her husband for a long time but finally she told Michelle that she could go home. Back in her village, Michelle was determined that her experience in Saudi Arabia should not be made known to anyone. Acutely conscious of having been detained in the police station and of the time she had spent in the shelter home, she had not even shared them with her husband and children. Michelle had no personal ties with Rajan but she too had concealed information about her plans to go to Saudi Arabia from her family and friends. After her return, Rajan had stopped answering her calls but Michelle refused to consider filing a case of extortion against him. She said she would wait for the two young women to return to sort out issues with him.

Discussion

I refer to the process of recruitment of domestic workers under the current regime as clandestine to direct attention to a specific mode of recruitment but also to the conditions that undergird it and make it possible. Clandestine recruitment is characterized by proactive facilitation and subterfuge, and though not unknown earlier, it may have gained traction under the current regime. At the local level, recruiters are bolstered by the patronage of political parties and law enforcement agencies. Owing perhaps to the entrenched nature of unauthorized recruitment, despite differences in state policy between 2014 and 2017, similar methods are used to recruit workers to Kuwait and Saudi Arabia. Recruiters continue to manipulate procedures through pushing or use visit visas. Notably then airports in Nagpur and Ahmedabad were used to send women from distant Trivandrum.[41]

Reetha's and Michelle's recruitment reveal how regulation works at the local level. Women are not immured from general information about overseas employment including deception by recruiters, the harsh conditions of work and possibility of abuse which circulate widely in the sending regions. Emigrant domestic workers say that they encounter abuse also from employers in India and preventing their recruitment only restricts their options. Their aspirations are honed on the many examples of women who have done well in the Middle East. Michelle expected to earn nearly four times the wage she received from a regular job as a domestic worker in the convent in her village.

A section of women like Michelle chose to seek overseas employment despite previous experience of such employment. An opaque regulatory environment makes it difficult for women to seek correct procedural information openly and to avoid the rotten elements. Recruiters manipulate the

---

[41] A number of women Trivandrum who were recruited in 2015–2016 went from Nagpur. Information SEWA activist.

fears of prospective clients, misinform them and take possession of their travel documents, which makes it difficult for women to cross-check information with other people. Prospective clients come under subtle pressure to conform to a pattern of behaviour that isolates them from their families/communities and generates dependence on recruiters.[42]

While the policy regime yields space to multiple and contrary voices, women emigrants experience its effects as oppressive. Women may find ways of surviving abuse but they are torn apart when they are not paid for their work. Recruiters expect women, once they are in the destination, to tolerate exploitation and a degree of abuse. This expectation may be founded at one level on the pressure on women to recoup their financial investment mobilized often at high interest rates from moneylenders. But where women resist exploitation or seek their assistance, recruiters were not unwilling to use violent means to discipline them.

Manju's intervention in Michelle's story brings in an additional dimension as it indicates the multiple roles intermediaries may play to generate returns. Michelle had been released by her sponsor and from the embassy shelter. The demand for domestic workers in Saudi Arabia and the connection that intermediaries have with potential employers but also possibly connections they may have in the embassy made it possible for another section of intermediaries to offer to channel women like Michelle into re-employment. Women who continued to work did so at their own risk.

Thus, at every level, the regime serves to criminalize women emigrants while effectively protecting brokers and rent-seeking state actors. Brokers are protected by the connections they have with state actors. But Michelle's experience shows that criminalization and stigma combine to silence women which lends impunity to the slew of actors who profit from clandestine recruitment. Reetha's family was compelled to go public and to act against the agent because they feared the worst but the agent was not punished. Eventually, Laiju went to Kuwait and mediated with her employer. According to Reetha's family, she continues to work in Kuwait; she now receives her salary regularly.

---

[42] Discussion with returnee domestic workers who had been mobilized by SEWA in a highland village in Trivandrum. The workers spoke about their personal experiences at one-to-one meetings after the joint discussion where they discussed the issue generally. Sister Sally, the representative of the National Domestic Workers Forum in Trivandrum, noted that prospective emigrants are difficult to find because of secrecy.

Conclusion

Restrictions on the recruitment to the Middle East serve to assuage public opinion which is built on the assumption that women domestic workers are not fit physically or morally for overseas recruitment. However, the Indian state is also under pressure to allow recruitment at least tacitly when its other business interests are at stake. Women domestic workers lack collective voice and hence have no power to influence policy. It is a travesty that restrictions are justified on the basis of voices that presume to speak in their interests such as the National Women's Commission. The avowed policy stance of discouraging women domestics' migration allows the state additionally to desist from programmes that would skill women workers prior to departure and from establishing the necessary infrastructure for the protection of their rights in the destinations.

I have attempted to show how interest conflicts generate regulatory gaps, concede space to unauthorized recruitment and undermine the interests of women. Extreme restrictions confine recruitment to a small segment of clandestine operators but women are recruited not because they are naïve as is sometimes presumed but because of a social context that embeds a history of migration. Clandestine recruitment is conditioned on the one hand by interest conflicts that drive the state to adopt a tough rhetoric of protection and at the same time to concede regulatory gaps and on the other by social contexts that spur women's aspirations.

The closure of the legal route to Kuwait and the enforcement of the bank guarantee increased the cost of recruitment (for sponsors in the Middle East), while the mobility agreement with Saudi Arabia brought pressure on recruiters to supply women domestics. These factors have complicated the process of recruitment especially for recruiters and their clients.[43] But there is demand in the Middle East, a social infrastructure that aids recruitment between the sending and receiving regions (in networks and connections) and a complex nexus between networks of recruiters and rent-seeking state actors. The current regime has generated conditions in practice where only the most dubious players may be willing to operate and is complicit in protecting them and in criminalizing women.

---

[43] In East Godavari too, there had been instances of local pastors who were part of networks that exploited women who were poorly informed by eager to find employment in the Middle East (Kodoth 2016a).

References

Bhattacharjee. (2015, October 10). India moves to stop flow of housemaids to Saudi Arabia. *The Hindu*.

Castles, S. (2004). The factors that make and unmake migration policies. *International Migration Review, 38*(3), 852–884.

Chari, M. (2016, January 24). Banning women from working in the Gulf will lead to more trafficking, say activists, Scroll.in.

Daniel, G. (2015, November 5). Kuwait stops issuing visas to Indian domestic workers. *The Economic Times*, economictimes.Indiatimes.com.

Errichiello, G. (2012). Foreign workforce in the Arab Gulf states (1930–1950): Migration patterns and nationality clause. *International Migration Review, 46*(2), 389–413.

Fernandez, B. (2012). Traffickers, brokers, employment agents, and social networks: The regulation of intermediaries in the migration of Ethiopian domestic workers to the Middle East. *International Migration Review, 47*(4), 814–843.

Kader, B. A. (2016, October 4). India imposes curbs on recruitment of female workers. *Gulf News*, gulfnews.com.

Kodoth, P. (2016a). Structural violence against emigrant domestic workers and survival in the Middle East: The effects of Indian emigration policy. *Interdisciplinary Journal of Economics, 28*(2), 83–106.

Kodoth, P. (2016b). Gender in internal and international labour migration: Women's migration, social disadvantage and implications for social development. In K. Kannabiran & Asha Hans (Eds.), *India social development report* (pp. 264–277). New Delhi: Oxford University Press.

Kodoth, P. (2016c). Migration policies, employment choices and the vulnerability of South Indian domestic workers in the Middle East. In M. Agarwal, J. Wang, & J. Walley (Eds.), *The economies of China and India cooperation and conflict, Volume 3: Economic growth, employment and inclusivity: The international environment*. Singapore: World Scientific.

Kodoth. P., & Varghese, V. J. (2011). *Emigration of female domestic workers from Kerala: Gender, state policy and the politics of movement* (Working Paper No. 445). Trivandrum: Centre for Development Studies.

Mallick, A. (2017, May 15). The horror of India's slave trade: No one stops agents trafficking women to Gulf countries. *The News Minute*, http://www.thenewsminute.com/article/horror-india-s-slave-trade-no-one-stops-agents-trafficking-women-gulf-countries-61516.

Nair, P. R. G. (1998). Dynamics of emigration from Kerala: Factors, trends, patterns. In R. Appleyard (Ed.), *Emigration dynamics in developing countries, Volume II: South Asia* (pp. 257–291). Aldershot: Ashgate.

Oishi, & Lum. (1996). International migration of Asian women: Distinctive characteristics and policy concerns. In G. Batistella & A. Pagamoni (Eds.), *Asian women in migration*. Manila: Scalabrini Migration Centre.

Pattadath. B., & Moors, A. (2012). Moving between Kerala and Dubai: Women domestic workers, state actors and the misrecognition of problems. In B. Kalir, M. Sur, & W. Schendel (Eds.), *Mobile practices and regimes of permissiveness* (pp. 151–168). Amsterdam: University of Amsterdam Press.

Rajan, S. I., Varghese, V. J., & Jayakumar, M. S. (2011). *Dreaming mobility and buying vulnerability: Overseas recruitment practices in India*. New Delhi: Routledge.

Walton-Roberts, M. (2012). Contextualizing the global nursing care chain: International migration and the status of nursing in Kerala, India. *Global Networks, 12*(2), 175–194.

Weiner, M. (2007). International migration and development: Indians in the Persian Gulf. In P. C. Jain (Ed.), *Indian diaspora in West Asia: A reader*. New Delhi: Manohar Publishers.

CHAPTER 6

An Industry of Frauds? State Policy, Migration Assemblages and Nursing Professionals from India

V. J. Varghese

Nursing Recruitment Scam

The presently defunct Ministry of Overseas Indian Affairs (MOIA) issued an order on the 12th of March 2015, making the procedure of 'emigration clearance' mandatory for its citizens emigrating for employment as nurses to all countries designated as Emigration Check Required (ECR) ones.[1] The order also banned recruitment of nurses through private recruiting agents (RAs) and restricted the recruitment to state-run recruiting agencies, namely NORKA Roots and ODEPC, both which are based in the

---

[1] Ministry of Overseas Indian Affairs, Emigration Policy Division, F.No. O1-11012/10/2013/EP, March 12, 2015, https://www.mea.gov.in/images/pdf/9-nurses-recur.pdf, accessed May 24, 2017.

V. J. Varghese (✉)
Department of History, University of Hyderabad, Hyderabad, India

© The Author(s) 2020
M. Baas (ed.), *The Migration Industry in Asia*,
https://doi.org/10.1007/978-981-13-9694-6_6

state of Kerala.[2] This extraordinary move was provoked by the disclosure of a massive recruitment fraud, involving a number of RAs headquartered in the city of Kochi in Kerala and who were contracted to recruit nurses for Kuwait in early 2015. The fraud came to light following an Income Tax (IT) raid in an RA named Al Zafara Travels and Manpower Consultancy (AZTMC), followed by another one named Mathew International (MI), and leading to the seizure of a large amount of unaccounted money. Based on the information provided by the IT Department of the Central Bureau of Investigation (CBI), the federal investigative agency and the Interpol agency of India registered a case and swiftly conducted raids in eight more Kochi-based RAs that were allegedly involved in the same recruitment fraud. The fraud as it was exposed involved a scam of 3–4 billion Indian rupees, though some newspapers went so far to claim it the amount exceeded even five billion. The CBI investigations also revealed that there were multiple recruiting firms involved in the fraud, some of them with offices/agencies in cities such as Mumbai and New Delhi and in smaller towns in Kerala like Kottayam and Adoor.

In this chapter, I will provide a detailed analysis of this scam in order to show how the Indian state and its emerging migration industry, especially where it involves the growing migration of nursing professionals, are deeply entangled and produce an inherently murky field of migration rules and practices. Through a detailed discussion, I attempt to disentangle the complex and supple relationship between state policy and the migration industry in India. I argue that the linkage between the two is embedded in a broader terrain of negotiations beyond state and industry. It is important to situate mutations and adjustments in state policy and migration industry within changing historical contexts implicated by changing conditions, practices, arrangements, and players in constituting migration regimes. The governmental regulation of emigration from India and its migration industry has been guided by a duality right from colonial times, wherein the prime target of regulation has been low or unskilled emigrants. This chapter attempts to explain the reasons for changing long-held policy

---

[2] The ECR countries are (1) Afghanistan, (2) Bahrain, (3) Indonesia, (4) Iraq [presently suspended], (5) Jordan, (6) Kingdom of Saudi Arabia, (7) Kuwait, (8) Lebanon, (9) Libya [presently suspended], (10) Malaysia, (11) Oman, (12) Qatar, (13) South Sudan, (14) Sudan, (15) Syria, (16) Thailand, (17) United Arab Emirates, and (18) Yemen [presently suspended]. See, Emigration and You, Ministry of External Affairs, Government of India, http://www.mea.gov.in/Images/attach/20_Emigration_and_You.pdf, accessed April 10, 2018.

by bringing skilled nurses under the regulative framework. Besides this, it proposes to consider the migration industry as a situated, layered, and gerrymandering domain.

How Migration Fraud 'Works'

The scam involving the AZTMC was found to be a big-ticket fraud in terms of its magnitude. The RA in question had received a placement order from the Ministry of Health, Kuwait, to recruit 1400 nurses toward the end of 2014, and it had started the recruiting process by advertising in lead newspapers and conducting selection interviews in different cities. It had subsequently said to have collected around Rs. 2 million (approximately $30,000) as service charge from the selected candidates as against a permissible maximum of Rs. 20,000 (approximately $300).[3] Through its contract with the RA, the Kuwaiti health department (the employer) had authorized the latter to collect Rs. 19,500 from each recruits for the services extended. Though the money collected was almost a hundred times more than this, the recruits were given cash receipts for Rs. 19,500 only, apart from forcing them to provide an undertaking to the RA to the same effect. The candidates were made to pay the money once they cleared the test conducted by officials from the Kuwaiti Ministry of Health and before receiving the documents for migration and relocation.

By the time the CBI had registered a case against AZTMC on March 30, 2015, the RA had apparently recruited 800 nurses already and was in the process of relocating them to Kuwait in batches, though the RA had taken permission from the Protector of Emigrants (POE) for only 500 recruitments. Uthuppu Varghese, the proprietor of AZTMC, had flown out of India to Kuwait on 27 March, just before the case got formally registered and began to operate allegedly from Kuwait, Dubai, and Abu Dhabi. The selected candidates who had paid up already or committed to doing so by surrendering their educational certificates and blank cheques were happy that they were being moved to Kuwait, while many others were visiting the office regularly with money and documents to know the status of their application. Mathew International, the other RA involved, had also been accused with similar charges though was contracted for recruitment

---

[3] According to the rule, the charges that a recruiting agent in respect of services renders could be 'equivalent to wages for 45 days as per the employment contract subject to maximum Rs. 20,000'.

of only 400 nurse by the Kuwait Ministry.[4] It was found later that MI did not have a direct contract, but instead a subcontract for recruiting this number via another RA namely 'Munawara Associates' in Mumbai. Another recruiting agency called JK International also recruited for Kuwait, offering around Rs. 2 million as annual salary. The Pan Asia Tours and Travels Changanacherry and Trust International Adoor, both located in Kerala and blacklisted by MOIA, were also conducting recruitment, and all of them together have done reportedly around 1600 recruitments by the time the fraud surfaced.

More Than Extortion and Misappropriation

The case involved much more than extortion of money and appropriation of certificates and valuable securities from the aspiring nurses. In fact, a major portion of the defrauded money had allegedly been transferred to Kuwait and Dubai through *hawala* channels, with the assistance of two forex agents.[5] Suresh Babu, the owner of Suresh Forex in Kottayam, and K Abdul Nasser who ran the Malabar Foreign Exchange in Kochi had reportedly sent four billion rupees through such channels to the Gulf, Kuwait and Dubai in particular. Many of the recruits who were unable to pay the money in full had agreed to make the remaining payment in Kuwait after they commenced their jobs and started receiving salaries.[6] The money being siphoned off to the Gulf through informal networks and the money laundering it implies certainly point at the flourishing business that people like Uthup Varghese were involved in. The money might have either shored up their capital in their expanding business interests or might have offered pecuniary benefits for those who ensured the recruitment contract in the destination. The response of the Government of India was extraordinary; it went beyond the existing ECR regime by bringing the recruitment of

---

[4] Mathew International, established in 1974, with its Headquarters in Mumbai, India, is one of the pioneers of overseas recruitment and manpower placements and held a good portion of the Mumbai's overseas recruitment when Bombay was the hub of recruitment. It expanded over time and Kerala remains one of their key catchment areas, with an office in Kochi.

[5] *Hawala*, meaning transfer or trust, in its classic form is an informal system of money transfer across national borders and is largely trust driven. Of late, the system and its network are getting significantly formalized. See 'How hawala money-transfer schemes are changing', *The Economist*, October 15, 2015, https://www.economist.com/blogs/economist-explains/2015/10/economist-explains-12, accessed April 15, 2018.

[6] Signed blank cheques and stamp papers were extracted from them as securities.

professional nurses under extensive regulation and banning recruitment by private RAs.

Emigration Governance in India and Its Discontents

Governmental regulations of emigrations from India have so far focused almost exclusively on un- or low-skilled migrant workers. Build up largely on the Emigration Act of India 1983, enacted following a Supreme Court directive by an otherwise lukewarm government of Independent India for this kind of regulation, the institutional framework initially left the "skilled" or "professional" emigration from its regulation, based on a conjecture of protection by exception. In principle, this entailed a form of positive discrimination for ensuring the protection and support to the most vulnerable categories of aspirants to overseas employment.

Such an institutional framework has been molded largely by selectively copying the British colonial model of emigration governance in India. Though colonialism created conditions for emigrations from India, in an unprecedented scale and variety, the passport regime and the emigration regulations brought in place were based on differential treatments of subjects, wherein factors such as race, education, loyalty, social and economic position, and labor skills played defining measures of citizenship and prospects for mobility. The British Indian passport, introduced in the nineteenth century, assured protection of the British crown to its holder, but was a privilege available only to men of superior credentials in terms of means, education, and social position who could potentially be accepted as immigrants anywhere in the empire including colonies earmarked for white settlers (Lake and Reynolds 2008; Singha 2006; Huttenback 1973; Mongia 1999, 2007). It proved to be a convenient tool in the hands of the British to enforce loyalty from the native elites and disciplining the nationalist leadership, while men of humbler backgrounds were denied with official documentation for moving abroad other than tropical colonies (Metcalf 2005; Singha 2006).

The vast majority of emigrations from colonial India, including the indentured 'coolie' migrations, took place without an actual passport. Though terms like 'emigrate,' 'emigration,' and 'emigrant' were referred primarily to indicate indentured labor emigration in colonial India, and amounting to 1.3 million between 1830 and 1920 according to some estimates, indenture emigration was allowed on a documentary exercise called the 'coolie agreement' (Singha 2006). In reality, this did not provide any security to the coolie, instead of binding the laborer for five years with a particular plantation owner and to stagnant wages (Mongia 2007; Metcalf 2007; Singha 2006; Anstey and Anstey 1977). In the wake of sustained criticism against indenture as turning into a new system of slavery, the colonial government put in place a series of new regulations, which included the establishment of the office of the POE and a licensed recruitment regime (Tinker 1974; Lal 2006; Rajan et al. 2011). But coolie migrations were just a small part of the many types of emigrations from colonial India. 'Free' migration was taking place to nearby colonies such as Ceylon, Burma, and Malaya particularly from South India without any documentation whatsoever (Lal 2006; Bhaskar 2000; Ramasamy 1992; Guilmoto 1993; Lal 2006; Peebles 2001; Carter 1995), apart from diverse flows of other kind along the axis of labor, skills, and capital. All of such emigrations were taking place without a passport as an expression of citizenship and promise of protection, something which only changed confronted with the large-scale repatriations during the Great Depression (Metcalf 2007; Lal 2006). The Passport Act of 1920 along with the Emigration Act of 1922 put a stop to indentured labor emigration, a development which was influenced by an elite nationalist campaign in India for its abolition as well as the 'broken promise' of imperial citizenship, though retrieving India's 'national prestige' and stimulating national industrial development may also have played a role here (Shirras 1931; Singha 2006; Metcalf 2007; Mongia 2003).[7]

After Indian independence, there was sustained emigration to the West and subsequently to the Middle East as well. However, it was only in 1983 that the government of India enacted a new legislation and started building up institutional structures accordingly to govern emigrations from the country.[8] Though the immediate provocation was the Supreme Court directive as part of a judgment (Kangra and Others vs. Union of India, March 20, 1979) to systematize emigration and to regulate recruiting agents faced with increasing complaints of cheating and exploitation, the emergence of a robust overseas recruitment sector in response to the Gulf boom and the increasing volume of inward remittances to the country also arguably enabled this delayed interest (Varghese and Rajan 2012). This led

---

[7] The Act of 1922 specified procedures for emigration and steps to be taken by foreign agents in India for the welfare of such emigrant workers, apart from making government notifications mandatory for recruitment and emigration.

[8] An office called 'Controller General of Emigrants' in the Ministry of External Affairs was supposed to work broadly on the principles laid down by the colonial Emigration Act of 1922.

to the re-designation of the Controller General of Emigrants to the Protector General of Emigrations (PGE), with new responsibilities and powers. The new office got attached to the Ministry of Labour, till it was transferred to the MOIA in 2004 and to the Ministry of External Affairs (MEA) in 2016,[9] and since then, the emigration process, including protection and welfare of emigrants and the regulation of the recruitment practices and migration industry in the country, became the responsibility of the PGE.

THE EMIGRATION ACT AND TWO TYPES OF PASSPORT

India's Emigration Act of 1983 instituted the system of 'emigration clearance' with a stated intention of protecting Indians migrating abroad for employment. However, it was implemented by categorizing passports into two types; it was made mandatory only for ECR passport holders, leaving their Emigration Check Not Required (ECNR) counterparts out of the regulative framework.[10] Furthermore, emigration clearance was required only while travelling to ECR countries. The so-called ECR passports are provided to low-skilled, professionally ill-equipped and/or lesser- or uneducated citizens. Citizens who were graduates and above were initially exempted from this until the requirement was lowered to the Intermediate (higher secondary) level and then to the matriculation (secondary school) level. The creation of two types of passports and making emigration clearance binding only for ECR passports could be seen as an measure of governmentality,[11] as it is based on an assumption that less educated passport holders, aiming low-/unskilled jobs overseas, requires additional

---

[9]The formation of the 'MOIA' in September 2004 could be seen as a testimony of Government of India's growing interest in the affairs of overseas Indians. It got merged with the Ministry of External Affairs in January 2016, with a stated reason of avoiding duplication of work and improving efficiency.

[10]The PGE administers the through field offices called Protectors of Emigrants (POE) located in the seven cities originally, subsequently increased to ten. They are Chandigarh, Madras, Delhi, Hyderabad, Calcutta, Bombay, Cochin and Trivandrum, and recent additions being Jaipur and Raibareli.

[11]Governmentality combines government and rationality in it and, according to Michael Foucault, is the "art of government" that include a wide variety of control techniques by a 'liberal state' seemingly for the benefit of the people and with their consent. It is governing people through positive means to generate willingness of individuals to participate in their own governance (Foucault 1991).

protection due to their innate vulnerabilities and lack of capability to protect themselves (Varghese 2018).

The ECR passport holders wanting to emigrate for work abroad are thus deemed eligible for protection once she/he gets the emigration clearance. They have to submit their application to the POE either directly or through registered recruiting agents, supported by a specified set of documents (MOIA 2006).[12] After checking the application and ascertaining the veracity of documents submitted, the POE grants 'emigration clearance' to the intending emigrant.[13] In addition to this, the Act has also introduced a licensed recruitment regime. The PGE issues the Registration Certificates to the RAs after detailed screening of the applications for license, the requirements of which has been tightened with the passage of time in terms of norms, security deposits, service charges, and the powers of the PGE to suspend or cancel the registration of certificates of RAs if the latter violate the terms and conditions of the registration certificate.[14] The Act also provides space for direct recruitment by foreign employers, provided they obtain due permission from the respective Indian Mission or from the PGE to do so.[15]

However, the institution of emigration governance is marred by problems at the doctrinal and practical levels. While it has proved to be discriminatory as it has institutionalized two types of passports and accordingly marked its citizens, the promise of protection has also proven to be an empty one, absent in practice. Moreover, at times, exceptional procedural hurdles have been created against the most vulnerable sections of

---

[12] Till late 2007, the ECR passport holders had to get their ECR status suspended by the POE for even visiting any of the ECR counties. Unlike individual submissions, the RAs are required furnish additional documentation including demand letter, power of attorney from the employer, and employment contract, besides indemnity bond (upon the discretion of the POE) and a duly sworn in affidavit (see Rajan et al. 2011).

[13] The POE is empowered to reject an application for emigration clearance on various grounds; see Rajan et al. (2011, 33–34).

[14] See for the terms and conditions of the Registration Certificate, Emigration Rules, 1983, Section 10; and for the grounds on which registration may be suspended or cancelled, Emigration Act of 1983, Chapter III, Section 14. The Emigration (Amendment) Rules, 2009, has made a few timely amendments to it. There are 1187 registered and active recruiting agents functioning in India as of September 21, 2018; see https://emigrate.gov.in/ext/openPDF?strFile=RA_LIST_REPORT.pdf, accessed September 21, 2018.

[15] In case of exploitation of Indian workers, upon recommendation from the respective Indian Missions, the PGE could also place any foreign employer or Company under the 'Prior Approval Category' (PAC).

society in the name of protection; the case of unskilled/low-skilled female migrants, especially those who emigrate as domestic servants, is a case in point (Kodoth and Varghese 2012; Kodoth in this volume). Such measures engendered tensions with the receiving countries often, though was justified as an outcome of India's growing concern toward its emigrant workers (Thiollet 2016, 16–17). Instead of enabling, emigration clearance procedure has thus proven to be disabling and the ECR status has become a stamp of the vulnerability for its holder.

The Digitalization of Emigration Clearance Procedures

Since the last decade, the government of India has employed new technologies, leading to the automation of POE offices and the digitalization of emigration clearance procedures, something that has been justified on the grounds of bringing greater efficiency and transparency. The old emigration clearance stamp has been replaced with an electronically generated sticker, and the application process needs to be made online alongside the entire course of emigration clearance. Apart from the general shift of enlisting technology for migration governance, the move has been prompted by the substantial increase in the volume of migration, remittances, and the dramatic growth of private brokerage. In further advancement of its policy of digitalization of governance with the help of virtual technologies, the government of India very recently launched an e-platform, called *eMigrate*, for online solutions to emigration for employment.

Accordingly, an emigrant who has an ECR passport and intends to emigrate for work to any of the ECR countries has to apply through *eMigrate*. On reception of application, it will be processed online by the POE office in jurisdiction and the applicant will then be issued with an electronic emigration clearance if successful. The applicant has to upload the required documents online, apart from paying the fee and purchase the PBBY insurance via the same platform.[16] On completion of the online application, the applicant receives a digital Application Reference Number (ARN) and the option of downloading a PDF version of the application and payment receipt. All this can also be facilitated by approved RAs.[17]

In an attempt to empanel foreign employers recruiting Indian workers, these prospective employers are asked to register themselves on the *eMigrate* portal and approval is made subject to the clearance from the

---

[16] The documents include (1) Demand Letter, (2) Employment Contract, (3) Copy of VISA, (4) Copy of first page and last page of passport, (5) Emigrant photograph, (6) Copy of Aadhar Card (mandatory in case UID is entered in the emigrant registration form), (7) Copy of PBBY policy, (8) Copy of Rs. 20 lakhs life insurance policy (mandatory in case destination country is Libya), and (9) Affidavits, as applicable as per the jurisdiction POE office.

[17] https://emigrate.gov.in/ext/home.action.

respective Indian diplomatic mission. Only registered employers will be able to raise demand and apply for permits for recruiting Indian emigrants. The company in question is required to submit documents such as a specimen contract, certificate of incorporation, Registration of Company (RoC), and certificate to import manpower. Before providing clearance, an official from the Indian Mission may visit the company for further verification. On approval, a system-generated mail containing a unique employer id, a printable confirmation letter with bar code, and a password for accessing *eMigrate* system will be sent to the employer. The RAs also have to place their application through *eMigrate* for a variety of things such as applying for registration, Registration Certificate (RC) renewal, duplicate RC, RC cancellation/bank guarantee release, declaring closure of branch offices, applying for change in directors/partners, applying for addition of new branch offices, applying for change in office status, applying for change in profile details, acknowledging demand from employer, applying for interview/advertisement, applying for Emigration Clearance, and payment-related processes. It also allows to pay fee online for services and applications. Similarly, it allows foreign recruiting agencies to register in the *eMigrate* system and conduct recruitment in the stipulated manner. Moreover, the platform also offers different stakeholders the opportunity to network and share information on overseas recruitment and placement.[18]

However, the new requirements and bureaucratic processes are primarily applicable to workers who have the ECR stamp in their passports. It was supposed to bring greater transparency in the recruitment procedures and eliminate exploitation of employees and RAs. Even after switching to a digitally driven emigration clearance system, it is largely a document verification exercise and the POEs have no reliable mechanism to scientifically verify the documents. Often documents are forged and the nexus between corrupt RAs and government officials compounds the problem. There are innumerable occasions in which POEs themselves are caught on corruption charges of colluding with RAs for pecuniary benefits. The office of the PGE itself coming under investigation has not been rare, the most tragic of such incidents happening in 2009 when the then PGE under CBI investigation went into depression and killed five of his family members before killing himself (Das 2009). Moreover, the promise of protection as encapsulated in the mechanism of emigration clearance is not translated into reality as

---

[18] All information from *eMigrate* platform, https://emigrate.gov.in/ext/home.action.

the government of India hardly has any effective mechanism at the destination countries to protect migrant workers on the face of various distresses. Moreover, as 'protection by exception' is fundamentally discriminatory and in practice disabling, such emigrants and aspirants find it easy to rely on informal channels to emigrate by circumventing the legal route, via forgery of documents and the practice of 'pushing.' This allows the ECR passport holders to pass airport emigration checks without the necessary documentation and emigration clearance (Radhakrishnan 2010; Rajan et al. 2011; Varghese 2018).

The focus of India's emigration governance has thus been on the ECR category in particular. The response of the Indian state to the case of recruitment fraud described in the beginning could therefore be read as an extension of control to hitherto unregulated spheres. All nurses possessing a certificate recognized under the Indian Nursing Council Act of 1947 had been exempted from emigration clearance till said incident.[19] The extension of the regulative framework to include the professional category of nurses, an important conduit of emigration that provides mobility to young women, points to an actively flexible, watchful, and responsive state. However, the state is just one player involved here and it influences the responses of other players as much as being influenced by them, something which determines the disposition of the sector as a whole. The migration industry and its practices are ever-changing and always in the making. At any given time, it is constituted by multiple players, diverse interests, and intertwining practices; an outcome of what could be called as migration assemblage. It encompasses multiple actors and rationalities which are in productive tension with each other. It therefore escapes reduction of singular logic and assumes newer configurations with change of time and space (Ong and Collier 2008). The move to incorporate skilled and professional categories of migrants into the regulatory framework will arguably resulted out of reconfigurations of the migration assemblage, rather than a spontaneous, ethically determined and an essentially corrective state response to the recruitment scam in question.

---

[19] See *Emigration and You*, Ministry of External Affairs, Government of India, http://mea.gov.in/images/pdf/emigration_and_you_new.pdf, accessed March 15, 2018.

The Outmigration of Nurses from India

While being one of the major suppliers of nurses to the global healthcare market together with the Philippines, India is said to be running short of at least 2 million nurses at the moment (Walton-Roberts et al. 2017; Senior 2010). While the developed world attracts nurses from other countries with better remuneration, working conditions, and scope for professional growth, developing countries are unable to compete due to their inadequate public spending on health and a private healthcare industry with asymmetrical access and outcomes (Bank and Thorat 2015; Joumard and Kumar 2015; Senior 2010; Radwan 2005). The actual availability is estimated at 61.3 nurses per one lakh population in India, but with extremely askew distribution across the country (Anand and Fan 2016, 9–10). While districts with the lowest density of nurses are all located in the states of Bihar, Uttar Pradesh, and Jharkhand and the highest density districts are either in Kerala or are in state capitals or in the national capital, as many as 73 districts had no qualified nurses at all (Anand and Fan 2016, 80–84). The *High level expert group report on universal health coverage for India* has estimated the HRH density in India as of 2011 at 12.9 health workers per 10,000 population, of which only 5.4 were actual nurses (HLEG 2011). The preference of employment in urban areas, inadequate opportunity in the public sector, and low wages compounds the problem. Public health spending in India is exceptionally low with just around 1% of the country's gross domestic product (Kalra 2015).[20]

The shortage of supply remains a major policy and sector concern. Ironically, despite deficient supply, nursing is one of the most underpaid jobs in India today. In private sector hospitals, reportedly salaries range from Rs. 5000 to Rs. 10,000 per month (Gill 2016). The recently held strike by nurses in the state of Kerala under the banner of United Nurses Association (UNA) has brought to light the deplorable life of nurses employed with private hospitals in the state—most of them are said to be earning only Rs. 300–400 per day in a state where ordinary wage laborers earn Rs. 700–900 for a day's work. In the government sector as well, nurses are paid humiliatingly low amounts (Venkat et al. 2017). The gross mismatch between the rhetoric of being referred to as *white angels* and the actual financial compensation for work is appalling and continues to be the norm despite

---

[20]For a comparative understanding, this is 3% in China and 8.3% in the United States (Kalra 2015).

a Supreme Court appointed special committee in 2016, directing all state governments to ensure a basic salary consistent with what a nurse gets in the government sector in private hospitals with more than 50 beds (Nair 2017). The lack of social respect for nursing as a profession in India adds to the problem here. Affluent middle-class families and promising students remain disinterested in the profession, while those who do become nurses report suffering from ill treatment by patients, their relatives, and society in general (Nair 2012; George 2000).

Migration to foreign countries thus becomes a genuine consideration for many nursing professionals. Not only does this hold the lure of higher salaries but also better treatment, concomitant working atmosphere, and chances for career growth and socio-economic mobility. As a result, the vast majority of nurses in India aspire to be employed abroad (Percot 2006). Those who migrate to OECD countries enjoy much better social status and economic capability compared to not only nurses working in India, but also their counterparts migrating to Gulf countries (Percot 2006). However, these female nurses often strategies their movement from one space to the other by taking advantage of the new opportunities and experience gained over time and as a result many often migration to the Gulf would be the first step for an eventual resettlement in the West (Percot 2006).

The migration industry that has emerged as a result of such mobility desires has undergone a significant amount of commercialization in recent times, particularly with regard to the movement to OECD countries. New Delhi, Bangalore, and Kochi have emerged as the three major recruiting hubs (SLD and NGA 2013; Khadria 2007). Some Indian corporate hospitals have begun 'business process outsourcing' (BPO) to take advantage of the phenomenon of increased demand for quality and trained nurses in the developed world and the desire of Indian nurses to seek employment outside the country (Khadria 2007). They recruit and train Indian nurses in their hospitals located in the metropolitan cities of India and prepare them to take the qualifying professional and language proficiency examinations. Delhi-based agencies recruit from across the country and tend to focus on the U.S. market, while those in Kochi and Bangalore are mainly facilitating migration of nurses to other destinations such as the Gulf countries, Australia, New Zealand, Singapore, Ireland, and the United Kingdom (SLD and NGA 2013; Khadria 2007). The major players are Max HealthStaff, Western International University (Mody Private group), Escorts Heart Institute, the Apollo Hospitals, and Jaipur Golden Hospital, with many of them having tie-ups with big healthcare groups in the respective countries (Khadria 2007; SLD and NGA 2013; John 2007). The United States and United Kingdom have been the most preferred destinations for migration for nurses, followed by Canada, Australia, and New Zealand (SLD and NGA 2013). But most migrating nurses from India choose countries closer to their home like those in the Gulf, though the migration to farther geographical regions is on the rise (Blythe and Baumann 2009; Percot 2006; Ross et al. 2005; Spetz et al. 2014). While BPOs operate for OECD countries, conventional RAs look for business in locations like the Gulf, where they get contracts often through negotiations and back door maneuverings.

The Aftermath of the Nursing Recruitment Fraud

The nursing recruitment fraud discussed earlier allegedly involved the full knowledge and connivance of the (POE) in Kochi at that point in time. In fact, the first accused in both the charge sheets submitted by the CBI is Lawrence Adolphus, the then POE in Kochi.[21] The POE was arrested in June 2015, for allegedly abetting extortion of money by the RAs involves from nursing recruits to Kuwait. The CBI found POE acting hand in glove with a number of recruiting firms and agents, which includes a few agents without even valid license for overseas recruitment. It is clear that he POE was fully aware of the scam, but chose to willfully ignore it, allegedly by accepting a handsome bribe. The investigating team had found that at least one complaint had been filed against the recruiting firm in question with the POE, who not only did not act, but even sent copy of the complaint to the same firm, with which the latter threatened the complainant and forced her to withdraw the same.[22] Though the MOIA suspended the tainted officer on his arrest and remand, the MEA delayed a nod to prosecute the POE as requested by the CBI after completing the probe for almost one year.[23]

---

[21] FIR No. RC 5(A)/2015- CBI/Cochin, registered by the CBI.

[22] 'CBI files the charges: How Kerala's nurses were ripped off by consultants,' *Indian Express*, January 21, 2017, http://www.newindianexpress.com/states/kerala/2017/jan/21/cbi-files-the-charges-how-keralas-nurses-were-ripped-off-by-consultants-1562063.html, accessed May 15, 2017.

[23] 'Ten months on, MEA nod awaited to prosecute protector of emigrants in nursing scam,' *Indian Express*, January 21, 2017, http://www.newindianexpress.com/states/kerala/2017/jan/21/ten-months-on-mea-nod-awaited-to-prosecute-protector-of-emigrants-in-nursing-scam-1561894.html, accessed May 15, 2017.

The inordinate delay has provided space for the prime accused to get his suspension revoked and rejoin services.

The accused officer was originally a Section Officer in Ministry of Health and Family Welfare (MoHFW) in the Government of India and had joined as POE Cochin on transfer on loan basis. He was arrested on June 15, 2015, and was in CBI/Judicial custody till July 29, 2015, and consequently placed under suspension with effect from June 15, 2015. The suspension was extended twice, for 180 days first and for another 90 days subsequently, despite his repeated appeals to the MOIA/MEA for getting reinstated in the services. The MEA instead canceled his transfer and repatriated the officer back to his parent Department. On MoHFW's refusal to accept his return for being in a suspension administrated by another Ministry, the former POE approached the Central Administrative Tribunal for restoring him in government service. The officer contended that till then no disciplinary proceedings were initiated; the CBI investigation has been lagging and may take 3–4 years to complete and that the continued suspension of the applicant is against the judgment of the Supreme Court reported in Ajay Kumar Choudhary v. Union of India and another (2015) 7 SCC 291. He also contended that the MEA has unduly delayed the sanction for prosecution sought by the CBI and the matter forgotten apparently due to merger of erstwhile MOIA and the MEA. Through O.A. No.180/00451/2016, December 7, 2016, the Tribunal has ordered to revoke the suspension of the former POE and directed him to report to MoHFW for joining after availing the permissible joining time of 15 days. The Tribunal also brought it to the notice of the appointing authority that 'in spite of the requisition for prosecution sanction having been made on March 11, 2016 no order has been issued on the same,' despite the 'seriousness of the allegations and the need for probity and accountability in public life.'[24] The case demonstrates that majority of erring officials make their way back to the services by making use of the available redressal mechanisms and laxities in penalization and remain largely unaffected by the corruption charges, arrest, suspension, and litigation.

---

[24] All these information is taken from the Central Administrative Tribunal, Ernakulam Bench Order (O.A. No.180/00451/2016), December 7, 2016, on the compliant of the said POE to revoke his suspension and reinstatement in service; https://indiankanoon.org/doc/119649230/, accessed May 20, 2017.

Corruption and Fraudulence in the Migration Industry

The Recruitment Agencies (RAs) involved in facilitating migration have been castigated time and again as the single most important reason for corruption and fraudulence in the sector and often the governmental interventions seek its justification from such an entrenched perception (Rajan et al. 2011). In reality, the erring RAs are making use of the institutional gaps or negotiate a space for informality with other stakeholders including government officials, where control and regulation become a precondition for informal practices (Kodoth and Varghese 2012). The present case too demonstrates how successful the RAs are in influencing government officials to their advantage and how government officials concede for their mutual benefit. The main RAs involved this case has strong connections beyond India and is part of a transnational network. Al Zarafa and Uthup Varghese's involvement also speaks volumes about how murky the dealings in the recruitment of skilled manpower are, something usually said to be associated only with the recruitment of un- or low-skilled labor. Finding himself in trouble, Uthup Varghese along with his wife, who happened to be the chairperson of the firm, reportedly escaped to Kuwait and were moving to other Gulf countries to evade arrest, irrespective of the Kerala High Court and the Supreme Court of India rejecting the anticipatory bail pleas. Only after the intervention of Interpol and a red corner notice, he could be apprehended in the Gulf and arrested in India. He has been charged with cheating, conspiracy with a public servant to commit criminal misconduct, and collection of excess service charge from emigrants, but managed to come out on bail sooner after the arrest and custodial interrogation. His *hawala* networks allowed him to transfer funds promptly and made it available where he wants it to be. But his experience with illegal activities allegedly has a longer history. In 2009, he was involved in an attempted murder case, after which he absconded to Afghanistan, remade himself in the Gulf, and then went on to establish a recruiting firm in Kerala.[25] His earlier experience with criminal activities, absconding to safer havens, building new networks and amassing wealth and experience in the Gulf proved seem to have to come in handy. The CBI was only able to arrest him only

---

[25] 'Kerala nursing recruitment scam: Uthup Varghese remanded in shooting case,' *Deccan Chronicle*, April 6, 2017, https://www.deccanchronicle.com/nation/crime/060417/kerala-nursing-recruitment-scam-uthup-varghese-remanded-in-shooting-case.html, accessed May 21, 2017.

after two years of registering the case.[26] The CBI also confirmed that he carried considerable influence with the Kuwait health ministry, resulting in gaining contracts for carrying out nursing recruitments, which he in turn subcontracted to different recruiting firms, including the one chaired by his wife.

All this underlines that the actual outcome of governmental regulations on the migration industry in sending locations depends substantially on the policies, practices, and players in the countries of destination as well. The GCC countries are moving to a model of issuing work visas through RAs and manpower companies based in those countries, through whom the RAs in the sending location obtain contracts often by making payments. Such a reciprocal and supportive network allowed Uthup to continue his business from Kuwait even after the case got registered and the red corner notice. In its argument against granting anticipatory bail to Uthup, the CBI informed the apex court that he 'was still collecting money and documents in Kuwait.'[27] Operating from Kuwait, he allegedly held recruitments in places like Dubai and Abu Dhabi, by collecting exorbitant amounts. The case also points to a robust recruitment market in India with large number of aspirants longing to emigrate, some of them reportedly even travelled to Dubai to attend the job interview.[28] Thousands appeared for the interview in Kerala and agreed to pay the hefty sums demanded and only one among them approached the POE with a compliant. None of the applicants complained to the police. They were even found to be mobilizing money from private moneylenders to realize their dream of becoming high-earning expatriate nurses in Kuwait. Uthup has even used this as a justification for his practices and has argued that there is no compliant against him by the recruits/candidates and that they have actually been placed as promised.[29]

---

[26] 'It was rags-to-riches for scam accused,' *The Hindu*, August 11, 2017, http://www.thehindu.com/todays-paper/tp-national/tp-kerala/it-was-rags-to-riches-for-scam-accused/article19469753.ece, accessed April 23, 2018.

[27] 'HC rejects bail plea of Uthup,' *The Hindu*, June 13, 2015, http://www.thehindu.com/news/cities/Kochi/hc-rejects-bail-plea-of-uthup/article7311805.ece, accessed May 23, 2017.

[28] http://www.iikwebadvt.com/ShowArticle.aspx?ID=36743&SECTION=0, accessed May 23, 2017.

[29] It is reported later that the recruited nurses did not get government jobs in Kuwait, instead are being accommodated in the school health program on a much lesser pay than the promised. See 'More than 800 recruited nurses are jobless in Kuwait,' *The Times of India*,

At the same time, the new formalization technologies faced backlash from the market, the fortified players and even the governments of destination countries. The market has been flagged this in terms of constituting 'excessive regulations' and even has referred to it as involving as torturous emigration policy. Some have even cut their recruitment from India in response. The percentage of jobs (newly) held by Indians in the Gulf has reportedly declined steeply after 2013. India held 57% of immigrant jobs in the Gulf in 2013, a number which declined to 44% in 2014 and then to 37%, 27%, and as low as 20% in subsequent years. Meanwhile, Bangladesh increased its share from 18% in 2013 to 51% in 2017, while Pakistan more or less retained its share (Nawaz 2017). The migration industry and the institutional support in competing markets also influence the functioning and opportunities of the migration industry and its associated migration assemblages. This was also seen as the reason for India's declining remittance over the last three years (69.8 billion in 2014, 68.9 in 2015, and 62.7 in 2016, though increased to 65 in 2017).[30] Moreover, there are governmental objections too. Recently, UAE has raised objections to India's *eMigrate* program citing issues of sovereignty. While India's attempt to create a database poses some concerns, the UAE has been seriously concerned about *eMigrate*'s mandate to inspect companies and their premises in UAE by Indian officials. Other Gulf countries including Saudi Arabia have raised similar concerns.

Conclusion

A mutually constituting relationship between state policy and migration industry could be postulated from the preceding discussion on India. The state is seen responding to emerging and deviant practices industry practices, while the industry and market remain in constant engagement with changing governmental interventions. Such a mutuality is entangled in a wider terrain of negotiations with impinging conditions and practices, together constituting the larger migration assemblages to which all of them

June 19, 2015, https://timesofindia.indiatimes.com/city/kochi/More-than-800-recruited-nurses-jobless-in-Kuwait/articleshow/47728151.cms, accessed April 28, 2018.

[30] Minister of State for External Affairs V. K. Singh in Rajya Sabha, reported in NDTC as 'India's Remittance Inflow Further Declines By $4.3 Billion In 2016–17,' NDTV, March 16, 2018, https://www.ndtv.com/india-news/indias-remittance-inflow-further-declines-by-4-3-billion-in-2016-17-1824471, accessed April 28, 2018.

are contributing as much as being shaped by them. The configuration and practices of the migration industry are thus determined by historically and institutionally situated migration assemblages, which is an outcome of constant and ever-changing interaction between heterogeneous actors such as the state(s), capital, market(s), public pressure, spaces available in the institutional structure, supply–demand dynamics, social networks, and formal and informal brokers and on local, national, and transnational scales, apart from governmental policies in the sending, destination, and competing locations. The experience so far reveals that the expansion of the regulative infrastructure, stringent 'migration policing', and new operational mechanisms based on virtual technologies have not really impacted the political economy of corruption/frauds in a positive way. Instead, control has become a precondition for informality, wherein players within the state apparatus and illegal actors are seen brokering meeting grounds to work around increased regulation. In such a state of controlled informality, stricter formal–informal dualism is neutralized and fluid practices abound in ductility (Kodoth and Varghese 2012). Consequently, managing migration by losing sight of the migration assemblages and detaching it from competing state and market regimes is a near impossibility in the Indian case.

References

Anand, S., & Fan, V. (2016). *The health work force in India: Human resources for health observer series no. 16*. Geneva: World Health Organization.

Anstey, V., & Anstey, V. P. (1977). *The economic development of India*. New York: Arno Press.

Bank, D., & Thorat, A. (2015). Issues of unequal access to public health in India. *Frontiers in Public Health, 3,* 245.

Bhaskar, T. L. S. (2000). *The Telugu Diaspora in the United States*. CGIRS Working Paper Series—WP#2000-1.

Blythe, J., & Baumann, A. (2009). Internationally educated nurses: Profiling workforce diversity. *International Nursing Review, 56*(2): 191–197.

Carter, M. (1995). *Servants, sirdars and settlers: Indians in Mauritius, 1834–1874*. New Delhi: Oxford University Press.

Das, A. (2009, August 3). Will it help unearth the rampant trade in illegal emigration? *Current News*.

Foucault, M. (1991). Governmentality. In G. Burchell, C. Gordon, & P. Miller (Eds.), *The Foucault effect: Studies in governmentality* (pp. 87–104). Hemel Hempstead: Harvester Wheatsheaf.

George, S. M. (2000). *When women come first: Gender and class in transnational migration*. Berkeley: University of California Press.

Gill, R. (2016). Scarcity of nurses in India: A myth or reality? *Journal of Health Management, 18*(4), 509–522.

Guilmoto, C. Z. (1993, January 16–23). The Tamil migration cycle, 1830–1920. *Economic and Political Weekly*.

HLEG. (2011). *High level expert group report on universal health coverage for India*. New Delhi: Planning Commission of India, Government of India.

Huttenback, R. K. (1973). The British empire as a White Man's Country: Racial attitudes and immigration legislation in colonies of white settlement. *Journal of British Studies, 13*(1), 108–137.

John, S. (2007, March 11). Sunrise industry: Nursing a dream. *Times of India*. 2007. https://www.pressreader.com/india/the-times-of-india-new-delhi-edition/20070311/282282430842006. Accessed 28 March 2018.

Joumard, I., & Kumar, A. (2015). *Improving health outcomes and healthcare in India*. OECD Economics Department Working Paper No. 1184. http://www.oecd.org/officialdocuments/publicdisplaydocumentpdf/?cote=ECO/WKP%282015%292&docLanguage=En. Accessed 16 March 2018.

Kalra, A. (2015, February 28). India keeps tight rein on public health spending in 2015–16 budget. *Reuters*. https://www.reuters.com/article/india-health-budget/india-keeps-tight-rein-on-public-health-spending-in-2015-16-budget-idUSL4N0W20CA20150228.

Khadria, B. (2007). International nurse recruitment in India. *Health Services Research, 42*(3), 1429–1436.

Kodoth, P. This volume. Unauthorized recruitment of migrant domestic workers from India to the Middle East: Interest conflicts, patriarchal nationalism and state policy. In M. Baas (Ed.), *The Migration Industry in Asia* (pp. 77–107).

Kodoth, P., & Varghese, V. J. (2012). Protecting women or endangering the emigration process: Emigrant women domestic workers, gender and state policy. *Economic and Political Weekly, 47*(43), 56–66.

Lal, B. V. (Ed.). (2006). *The encyclopedia of the Indian diaspora*. Singapore: Singapore National University.

Lake, M., & Reynolds, H. (2008). *Drawing the global colour line: White men's countries and the international challenge of racial equality*. Cambridge: Cambridge University Press.

Metcalfe, T. R. (2005). *Forging the Raj: Essays on British India in the heyday of empire*. New Delhi: Oxford University Press.

Metcalfe, T. R. (2007). *Imperial connections: India in the Indian Ocean Arena, 1860–1920*. New Delhi: Permanent Black.

MOIA. (2006). *Handbook for Overseas Indians (HOI)*. New Delhi: Government of India.

Mongia, R. V. (1999). Race, nationality, mobility: A history of the passport. *Public Culture, 11*(3), 527–555.
Mongia, R. V. (2003). Impartial regimes of truth: Indentured Indian labour and the status of the inquiry. *Cultural Studies, 18*(5), 749–768.
Mongia, R. V. (2007). Historicizing state sovereignty: Inequality and the form of equivalence. *Comparative Studies in Society and History, 49*(2), 384–411.
Nair, S. (2012). *Moving with the times: Gender, status and migration of nurses in India*. New Delhi: Routledge.
Nair, N. (2017, June 30). Kerala nurses wage war against abysmal pay and government apathy; laugh indefinite strike. *Firstpost*. https://www.firstpost.com/india/kerala-nurses-wage-war-against-abysmal-pay-and-government-apathy-launch-indefinite-strike-3760655.html. Accessed 2 April 2017.
Nawaz, A. (2017, February 27). How India's recent migration policies helped Bangladesh and Pakistan to Eat into our GDP. *The Outlook*. https://www.outlookindia.com/website/story/how-indias-recent-migrant-policies-helped-bangladesh-and-pakistan-eat-into-our-g/298076. Accessed 3 May 2017.
Ong, A., & Collier, S. J. (Eds.). (2008). *Global assemblages: Technology politics and ethics as anthropological problems*. Oxford: Wiley-Blackwell.
Peebles, P. (2001). *The plantation tamils of Ceylon*. London: Continuum International Publishing Group.
Percot, M. (2006). Indian nurses in the Gulf: Two generations of female migration. *South Asia Research, 26*(1), 41–62.
Radhakrishnan, M. G. (2010, June 21). Kerala: Republic of Kasargod. *India Today*.
Radwan, I. (2005). *India: Private health services for the poor—A policy note*. Health, Nutrition and Population (HNP) Discussion Paper. Washington, DC: The World Bank.
Rajan, S. I., Varghese, V. J., & Jayakumar, M. S. (2011). *Dreaming mobility and buying vulnerability: Overseas recruitment practices and its discontents in India*. New Delhi: Routledge.
Ramasamy, P. (1992). Labour control and labour resistance in the plantations of Malaya. *Journal of Peasant Studies*. Special Issue.
Ross, S. J., Polsky, D., & Sochalski, J. (2005). Nursing shortages and international nurse migration. *International Nursing Review, 52*(4), 253–262.
Senior, K. (2010). Wanted: 2.4 million nurses, and that's just in India. *Bulletin of the World Health Organization, 88*(5), 327–328.
Shirras, F. G. (1931). Indian migration. In W. F. Willcox (Ed.), *International migrations volume II: Interpretations* (pp. 591–616). NBER.
Singha, R. (2006). A 'proper passport' for the colony: Border crossing in British India, 1882–1920. *Colloquium series, Program in Agrarian Studies*, Yale University. http://www.yale.edu/agrarianstudies/papers/16passportill.pdf. Accessed 5 February 2008.

SLD and NGA. (2013). *A Study on Migration of Indian Nurses to the OECD Countries: Trends and Challenges*. New Delhi: Society for Labour Development and National Guestworker Alliance USA.

Spetz, J., Gates, M., & Jones, C. B. (2014). Internationally educated nurses in the United States: Their origins and roles. *Nursing Outlook, 62*(1), 8–15.

Thiollet, H. (2016). *Managing migrant labour in the Gulf: Transnational dynamics of migration politics since the 1930s*. IMI Working Paper Series No. 131. University of Oxford.

Tinker, H. (1974). *A new system of slavery: The export of Indian labour overseas 1820–1920*. London: Oxford University Press.

Varghese, V. J. (2018, March 1). ECR Devoid of orange is still a deterring passport. *Kafila*. https://kafila.online/2018/03/01/ecr-devoid-of-orange-is-still-a-deterring-passport-v-j-varghese/.

Varghese, V. J., & Rajan, S. I. (2012). Broadening exchanges and changing institutions: Multiple sites of economic transnationalism. In S. I. Rajan (Ed.), *India migration report 2012: Global financial crisis, migration and remittance* (pp. 322–346).New Delhi and Abingdon: Routledge.

Venkat, T., Tadepalli, S., & Manuel, T. (2017, December 3). The life of labour: Nurses' strike broken after HC threat, 48000 workplace fatalities in India every year. *The Wire*. https://thewire.in/labour/nurse-strike-tamil-nadu-workplace-safety-labour-rights. Accessed 2 April 2018.

Walton-Roberts, M., Bhutani, S., & Kaur, A. (2017). Care and global migration in the nursing profession: A north Indian perspective. *Australian Geographer, 248*(1), 59–77.

Index

A
Abu Dhabi, 87, 111, 126
Adoor, 110, 112
Afghanistan, 110, 125
Australia, 26, 122, 123

B
Bahrain, 87, 98, 110
Bangalore, 91, 122
Bombay, 82, 83, 101, 112, 115
Borderland, borderlanders, 38, 40, 43, 46, 47, 51, 52
Brokerage, 2, 5, 6, 8, 12–15, 19–22, 26–28, 34–37, 39, 42, 47, 49, 51, 52, 61, 64, 80, 90
Brokers, 2, 3, 5–7, 11, 12, 15, 19–28, 34, 36–38, 41–44, 46–52, 59–61, 68, 74, 82, 83, 85, 87, 89, 90, 92, 99, 104, 128
Burma, 33, 114
Business process outsourcing (BPO), 122, 123

C
Calcutta, 115
Canada, 123
Central Administrative Tribunal, 124
Central Bureau of Investigation (CBI), 110, 111, 119, 123–126
Ceylon, 114
China, 121
Colonialism, 113
Controlled Informality, 128
Coolie migration, 114

D
Digitalization, 117
Domestic workers, 7, 37, 45, 61, 77–81, 84–86, 88, 92–99, 103–105
Dubai, 111, 112, 126

E
Ecological crisis, 16
eMigrate, 95, 98, 113, 116–120, 126, 127
Emigration Act of 1922, 114

Emigration Act of India 1983, 113
Emigration Check Not Required (ECNR), 77, 115
Emigration Check Required (ECR), 77, 78, 83, 85, 93, 94, 101, 109, 112, 115–120
Emigration clearance, 78, 85, 88, 90, 92–94, 97, 98, 101, 109, 115–120
Emigration governance, 93, 113, 116, 120
Emigration policy, 109, 127
Ensemble, 3
Excessive regulation, 127

F
Feminization of brokerage, 15

G
Gender, 5, 8
Governmentality, 115
Green Revolution, 17, 18
Guestwork, guestworkers, 34, 37–39, 47, 51, 53
Gulf, 61–63, 70–73, 97, 112, 114, 122, 123, 125, 127

H
Hawala, 112, 125
Healthcare industry, 121
Human smuggling, 4, 36, 38, 39, 47
Human trafficking, 37, 39, 43, 45, 52
Hyderabad, 90, 91, 97, 115

I
Illegality, 37, 38, 52, 53
Indentured migration, 113
India, 6, 8, 60, 61, 72, 79–81, 83–86, 94–99, 103, 110–117, 120–127
Indian Nursing Council Act 1947, 120
Indonesia, 5, 7, 8, 12, 16, 17, 19, 20, 22–24, 27, 96, 110
Indramayu, 5, 11–21, 23–28
Informal, 5, 8, 11, 13, 20, 22, 35, 39, 42–44, 51, 61, 62, 70, 82, 97, 112, 120, 125, 128
Informal networks, 88, 112
Insurance, 42, 48, 118
Interpol, 110, 125
Iraq, 110
Ireland, 122

J
Jaipur, 115, 122
Jordan, 110

K
Kafala system, 86
Karen (ethnic group), 6, 33–35, 39, 43–47, 51, 53
Kerala, 61, 80, 82, 84, 89, 91, 97, 101, 110, 112, 121, 125, 126
Kochi, 110, 112, 122, 123
Kottayam, 110, 112
Kuwait, 79, 81–84, 86–88, 95, 97–100, 103–105, 110–112, 123, 125, 126

L
Labour migration, 6, 35, 37, 42, 52, 81, 83
Lebanon, 110
Legalisation, 33, 35, 45, 47, 51–53
Legality, 35, 37–39, 41, 42, 47, 50–53
Libya, 110, 118

M
Madras, 91, 115
Malaysia, 18, 37, 63, 74, 110

Middle East, 3, 7, 8, 25, 60, 62, 63, 70, 71, 73, 74, 77–79, 81–88, 92, 94, 96, 97, 99, 103, 105, 114
Migrant loans, 59
Migrant workers, 5–7, 11, 21, 22, 27, 34, 37, 40, 45, 48, 60, 61, 64, 65, 67, 69, 71, 73, 74, 86, 87, 97, 98, 113, 114, 120
Migration assemblage, 8, 120, 127, 128
Migration frauds, 128
Migration infrastructure, 6, 34, 36, 37
Minimum government, 93, 95
Ministry of External Affairs (MEA), 71, 96, 115, 123, 124
Ministry of Health and Family Welfare (MoHFW), 124
Ministry of Overseas Indian Affairs (MOIA), 93, 94, 96, 109, 112, 115, 123, 124
Moneylenders, 92, 104, 126
Mumbai, 110, 112
Myanmar, 6–8, 33–35, 37, 39–42, 44–50

N
Nationalism, 7, 79, 113
Nationalist campaign, 114
New Delhi, 110, 122
New Zealand, 122, 123
NORKA Roots, 109
Nurses, 63, 81, 109–113, 120–123, 126

O
ODEPC, 109
OECD, 122, 123
Oman, 87, 88, 92, 95, 98–100
Overseas recruitment, 69, 93, 94, 105, 112, 114, 119, 123

P
Passport, 12, 34, 39–42, 48–50, 68, 77, 82–84, 90–93, 100, 101, 113–116, 118–120
Passport Act of 1920, 114
Patriarchy, 7, 78, 79, 84
Philippines, 18, 96, 121
Precarity, 5, 8, 13–17, 22, 23, 26–28, 34
Private brokerage, 117
Protection by exception, 113, 120
Protector of Emigrants (POE), 78, 85, 92–94, 97, 101, 111, 114–119, 123, 124, 126

Q
Qatar, 110

R
Raibareli, 115
Recruiting agents (RAs), 80, 85, 90, 92, 94, 95, 101, 109, 114, 116
Rice agriculture, 18

S
Saudi Arabia, 26, 79, 81, 88, 90, 95–99, 101–105, 110, 127
Singapore, 2, 6, 8, 26, 28, 59–63, 65–67, 69–74, 101, 122
Skilled migration, 73
Slavery, 96, 114
South India, 77, 78, 98, 114
South Sudan, 110
Sri Lanka, 71
State policy, 79, 103, 127
Sudan, 110
Supreme Court, 113, 114, 122, 124, 125
Syria, 110

T

Tamil Nadu, 6, 60, 61, 64, 68–70, 73, 74, 96, 100
Temporary migration, 78
Thailand, 6–8, 18, 33–35, 37–50, 52, 110
Trivandrum, 80–82, 86, 87, 98–104, 115

U

Unauthorized recruitment, 7, 79, 80, 92, 103, 105
Undocumented, 4, 6, 13, 20, 23, 33–35, 37–39, 43, 45–53
United Arab Emirates (UAE), 92, 98, 99, 110, 127
United Kingdom (UK), 122, 123
United Nurses Association (UNA), 121
United States of America (USA), 121, 123

V

Virtual technologies, 8, 117, 128

W

West Java, 5, 12, 17
White settlers, 113
Women migrants, 81, 82

Y

Yemen, 110

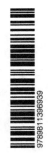